WHAT IT TAKES TO BE FREE

More from Darius Foroux

Win Your Inner Battles (2016)

How To Go From Procrastinate Hero to Procrastinate Zero (2016)

THINK STRAIGHT (2017)

Do It Today (2018)

The Road To Better Habits (2019)

Find them all at dariusforoux.com/books

WHAT IT TAKES TO BE FREE

DARIUS FOROUX

NORTH
EAGLE

CONTENTS

"Liberty is slow fruit. It is never cheap; it is made difficult because freedom is the accomplishment and perfectness of man."

— *Ralph Waldo Emerson*

INTRODUCTION

Freedom means living life on your terms. And if you picked up this book, freedom matters to you as much as it does to me. It's the highest form of success. Even though people are different and everyone desires different things, on a deeper level we share the same drive to be free.

Freedom means waking up in the morning and deciding exactly what you want to do that day. No unwanted obligations; no stress. Living free is not a fantasy. In our world everyone can live like that. The world is getting freer every day because of technology, which means we can work remotely and have unlimited access to information that improves our lives.

Even so, most of us are not free. More and more people feel crushed by the weight of obligations, debt, and social pressure. Most of us chase success without knowing what it looks like. To me, there's only one definition of success: **Freedom to**

live your life the way you want without hurting others. Success, or freedom, is not having a job with status, driving an expensive car, looking like a model, going on vacations, or living in a big house.

People who pretend you don't need much to be free are not being practical. Freedom isn't free. They might have a positive mindset, but in real life, we need more than positive thinking to actually be free. We need to build a life and career that allows us to be free. We also need money. That's why this book is highly practical and covers everything I've done to become free. Does my definition of freedom resemble yours? I doubt it, because remember, even though most people agree that freedom means being able to live your life the way you want, everybody wants different things.

That brings me to the first lesson I've learned about freedom: Do not feel guilty about what you want from life. In the past, I always felt pressured to want what others wanted. If your parents want you to become a doctor you think to yourself, "Should I become a doctor?" It's funny how that works. In reality, you don't want to become a doctor at all. You never even thought about becoming one. And yet, just because your parents want it for you, you give in.

It's the same thing with intimate relationships, which play a big role on the path to our freedom. When a girlfriend, boyfriend, partner, or spouse expects certain things from us, we often give in. We do things we don't want to do because we think it's better for the relationship. We do things that are out of our character. We lose face and, as a result, we become characterless. Is that freedom? Is that good for your relationship? No, of course not.

If these things are not bad enough, when it comes to our financial life, we're even worse off. Most of us spend too much, have debt, and have jobs we hate just to pay for a lifestyle we don't even like. What brought us to this point? We like nothing about our lives. It seems like we're trapped inside someone else's life. Every day is filled with unwanted obligations and tasks that make us miserable.

Freedom is the answer to all these things. But I have to tell you right now that the price of freedom is high. Living the way you want means suffering voluntarily. People will get upset with you, maybe even abandon you. You have to do hard things. But on the other side of suffering is freedom. It's a place very few people reach in life. Is it worth trying to get there? Absolutely. And if you're reading this book, you probably agree. Whether you're held captive by success or failure, I invite you to join me in freedom.

My journey began four years ago when I realized I wasn't free. It was a gradual realization. After living unfree my whole life, I woke up one day and thought to myself, "I don't want this life." It was a life of fake smiles, frustration, and captivity. I continuously gave into the requests of other people, my partner, family, job, and even society. We behave a certain way because we think that's how *we have to* behave. We have desires that we *think* we should satisfy—but is that really true? How often do you inspect your desires? Do you do what you do because YOU want to? Or, is it because you feel like you should do those things? And if it's the latter, where does that *should* come from?

Who ever said that we should do all the things we do? **You're free to do *anything* you want. That's obvious. But what's not obvious is why you're NOT doing what you want.** It has nothing to do with your status or intelligence. I know people who are considered successful in the eye of society, with a lot of money, respect, and wealth. But they are not free to do anything they want. They are a prisoner of their own success. Whether you're successful in the eyes of society or not, you probably know the feeling of being trapped.

How often does it happen that you start chasing something new? Think about a new job or career. Or maybe you want to live in a certain city. Maybe you want to find a romantic partner. You get something in your head, read a few books on conquering fear, get your act together and decide to pursue it. Congrats! You took action. But half way through, you realize you don't even want the thing you're chasing. But despite that realization, you put your head in the sand. You ignore the inner disturbance and keep going even though you don't want that thing anymore, that way of life. All of a sudden you feel restricted by all the obligations you've accumulated. You're trapped in a life you created.

Let's say you think you want to become successful in the city. You want to live a fast life, make money, go out, and have a fancy lifestyle. You pursue a business degree that helps you get into an organization that pays well. But during those four years in college you acquire debt. Now, you *have* to pursue a job that pays well, and a big paycheck is no longer a desire, it's a responsibility. Along the way you realize you don't want that lifestyle anymore. You hate the pressure, the people, the work, the parties—all of it. But you're already half way through so you think, "I can't quit. How could I pay the rent for my apartment in the city, my student debt, credit card debt, and car loan?"

Something like that happened to me. It's easy to get trapped. We also get easily trapped inside a romantic relationship. How often does it happen that two people grow apart? You or your partner change, and you no longer have the same values. The relationship only drains your energy because you're no longer compatible. And yet, you stay together. What's worse, you think buying a house and having kids will make everything better. The opposite is true.

You keep moving forward, while deep down, you want to live your life the way you want. But you can't because you're an unfree person living in a free world. You realize there's always a choice—a way out. You realize you *chose* to live a life you loathe. You've given up your desire to be free. Because no matter who you are or where you are, you have a desire to be free. We all have that desire. But we are trapped; trapped inside the limitations of our own minds. But we are also trapped by real things: Debt, obligations, responsibilities, and even people.

We can't accept these restrictions as facts. We need to break away from it all.

We need to become free. And we need to *stay* free.

It's not too late. It's *never* too late.

The Goal of This Book

Freedom means living your life the way you want. I will keep reminding you of this definition because the goal for this book is to help you achieve that within the next four years—just as I did.

My goal is not to convince you that my way of living is correct. I don't expect you to live your life the way I do. That would be insane. Everyone is different, and everyone wants different things. Most books ignore that and tell the reader, "This is the best way." I don't think there is such a thing. I can't tell you what to do. I will, however, share what I have done to become free. And I can point out all the ways you might be unfree right now.

You know ideas, self-talk, positive thinking and inspiration are cheap. It's all talk. This book is different. Everything you will read is based on what I've *done*. After finishing this book I hope you will have a plan to become free. And if you're already free, you can become freer. In this book I will explain how you can set yourself free from the most common traps of modern life. I don't have all the answers, but I will tell you everything

I've learned about being free. The goal is to live your life the way you want. But there's a price.

What does it take?

My goal is to be honest with you. And I'm certain you know that freedom comes at a price. If I pretended that freedom is easy to achieve, I would be a fraud. One of the most important things I've learned about freedom is that you must accept the truth. You are only responsible for yourself. When any decent human being tells a lie, either to himself or others, he will not be proud of it. When I lie, I can't look at myself in the mirror. Even though I value you, my reader, I value myself more than anything else in this world. That's the truth. If you can't take that, you probably won't finish this book. My philosophy for freedom is focused on the self. But it's far from selfish. As you read, I hope you realize why this is so. At the end of the book, I guarantee everything I've said will sound like common sense. You already know the things I will share with you. You also know that the people you love will be better off if *you* are happy and free. Deep down, we all have the same desires. This is your life, and you're responsible for your own well-being.

Ultimately, freedom gives you inner satisfaction, peace, and happiness. There's nothing like it. Before we get started, I want to ask two things of you:

1. **Be open-minded:** Some of the things I say in this book sound controversial or harsh. I ask you not to judge. I ask you to try these ideas and see for yourself. Ultimately,

every person has to decide for themselves what to do. You can accept or reject ideas.

2. **Actively read this book**: Be open to my way of living, but don't consider it the only truth. As you're reading this book, engage in a discussion. You can do that with yourself, inside your head, or in your journal. You can do that with me on social media. You can also bring up the topics in this book with the people in your life. I propose this way of reading because it's effective. It will help you get the most out of your time.

I can't guarantee you will be free within four years. But if you're committed to freedom, you will achieve it one day...if you're willing to pay the price.

What You Can Expect

Part I of this book is about awareness. What stands in the way of our freedom? There are so many traps we are unaware of. Why do we feel overwhelmed? Why do we dislike our work, relationships, and ourselves? Why do we end up in situations that seem hopeless? In Part I, I share the most important obstacles to freedom. In Part II, I share what I gave up to be free. We want it all. But the truth is we can't have it all. Should that be a problem? No, not at all. **It's actually liberating once you realize that you don't need to do everything. You can give up many things you're currently doing. And, as a result, you will become free.**

Part III is an action plan. I will share specific techniques that *prepare* you to become free. Ideas are great, but useless without execution. Life is full of challenges, and positive thinking alone will not help you—*but preparation will.* While your peers are questioning the meaning of life and dealing with personal crises, you will be free from it all. You will be prepared for all the big challenges of life. It might not seem like it when you're dealing with problems, but nothing is new. All problems have been faced by other people in the past. It's up to us to study everything that could go wrong in life, and then *prepare* for it.

That's the way to be truly free. Is it complicated? No. None of the ideas in this book are difficult. In fact, you will probably recognize most of the things I share. But remember that ideas by themselves are cheap. Your *execution* is what matters; it's the only thing that matters. And that's the hardest thing on the planet. But that shouldn't scare you because the reward is freedom—the highest aim in life.

"Is freedom anything else than the right to live as we wish? Nothing else."

— Epictetus

PART I

AWARENESS

"Expose yourself to your deepest fear; after that, fear has no power, and the fear of freedom shrinks and vanishes. You are free."

— Jim Morrison

CHAPTER ONE

WHAT IS FREEDOM?

Freedom is to do what you want and to be what you are. The problem is that we've created an unfree life for ourselves. I believe in a simple concept called personal responsibility. It means we are responsible for our own lives. We create our lives by the decisions we make. That means we have the power to live any way we want.

Why are we not using that power? There are many reasons for that. And we will cover them all in Part I of this book. To become free requires being aware of the things that limit our freedom. Without that awareness, I don't think we can ever be free. We need to confront ourselves with the utmost honesty. You probably won't like some of the things you'll read here. I certainly didn't when I discovered what restricts our freedom.

These traps are very real and exist in all of our lives.

But before we talk about those traps I want to define freedom beyond the definition I used at the beginning of this section. Freedom means living life the way I want. This is a subjective definition of freedom because "the way I want" is different for every person. Nonetheless, the interesting part about freedom is that most of us have the same ideas about being free:

- Doing work you enjoy
- Taking time off whenever you want
- Being yourself without being judged by others
- Not having to defend yourself
- Spending time with people you like

These things are universal. I've never met a person who didn't want freedom. However, there's a difference between what people want and what people do. Although many of us claim to have a desire for freedom; our actions do not reflect the pursuit of a free life. We take jobs we hate, we are in relationships with people we don't love, and we say yes to things we don't want to do.

As a result, we're tied down by obligations that make us miserable. It's the opposite of freedom. The reason we're unfree is because freedom is the most difficult thing in life one can achieve. That automatically makes it the noblest thing one can achieve. To say things like, "Being free is easier said than done" is to state the obvious. I can't relate to people who say that. What did you expect? That it was easy? Give me a break. Life is hard for every single person. "Yeah, but he's rich!" So what? "Yeah, but I'm a minority!" I am too. In fact, I've experienced discrimination on different occasions. So what? I'm not going to let that destroy me. Life isn't easy, no matter what your circumstances are.

I want you to accept that as you go on this journey. The majority of people will never achieve freedom. They are too weak. They give up quickly. And you should NEVER let these people hold you back. Because on the other side of this journey, freedom awaits. Picture this: You wake up whenever you want, drink a cup of coffee, eat breakfast with your family, and start working on something you love. After three hours of focused work, you check your email, watch or read something you're curious about, and then you put on your running gear to go for a run. You come back, take a shower, read a book on your sofa, and when you're tired, you take a nap.

You wake up, prepare dinner with your partner, eat, hang out on the couch, and watch a T.V. show. Maybe you talk to a friend on the phone and then do some more work. Before you go to bed you read again. By that time, your eyes want to close themselves. That's an average day for me.

You can create your own ideal day. If you have kids, you spend more time with them. If your elderly parents live with you, you spend time with them. If you have a dog, you hang out with your dog. You can do whatever you want. Life is meant to be enjoyed. Life is meant to be used. **When we're free, we use**

our time. We make ourselves useful to our community. That's ultimate freedom. Let's talk about the things holding us back from achieving that.

"To be free, you have only to make the decision to be free. Freedom is waiting for you—anytime you're ready for it."

— Harry Browne

CHAPTER TWO

NO CORE VALUES

Freedom starts with knowing who you are and what you want. This is your life, and you decide what you want to do with it— no one else *can* or *should* make that decision for you.

But if you have no core values, you're tossed around by life. Who are you? What do you stand for? What do you believe in? Only you can answer those questions. And you're free to do anything you want.

Most of us don't realize we have that power. We live our entire lives believing we have to obey others. We fear that if we don't obey people, they will be disappointed in us. Who cares? This is your life. And you have to feel good about it. You don't have to be happy all the time. But you do have to feel good about what you do. That's important to everybody on this planet. We all want to be happy and feel like we matter. What's the point of being happy but feeling useless? Selfish pursuit of happiness might feel good for a while, but sooner or later, we realize that life is not about us. People can only be happy and useful if they feel good about themselves.

But what if you don't know who you are? I think that's the biggest problem we have. We never think about what's important to us. We don't live consciously. We can only do that if we live by certain rules we set up for ourselves. Those rules are our values.

Understanding who you are and what you want is an ongoing process. It ends when life ends. You can never 100% know yourself. That's the most important thing about self-knowledge. If you think you know yourself, you have a long way to go. People change. If you commit yourself to a life of growth and freedom, you are not the person you were yesterday. Today is a new day. And today, you have the chance to be different.

Some people don't look at life that way. They believe people cannot change. "This is simply who I am." That's a pessimistic way to look at life. The way I look at life, I was worse yesterday. I was weaker and had less knowledge. That's because I learn every day. And my intention is to become better every day. So if you judge me based on my past actions, you're judging someone else. Today, you're a new person. People think life is static. And that you are what you are. But here's the thing: We don't know who we are. We have to uncover our values constantly. Having a static view of life is what makes people give up. "Well, there's nothing I can change about my life." That's not true. No matter where you are in life or what you do, you can ALWAYS do something about it. You have power. You can decide to do whatever you want to do.

But *what* do you want? If you don't know, figure it out as you read this book. View reading this book as an exercise that helps you find the way you want to live your life. Over the past four years, I've thought about that every day. Now, I know how I want to live my life. And more importantly, I know how I *don't* want to live my life. I don't want to be caged. I don't want to be afraid of what people think of me and my actions. I do what I want. And if people don't like it, I don't mind. I believe in freedom. Others can also do what they want. The important thing is that I have a set of core values I live by. That's how I make sure I don't end up in jail or alone, in a ditch. Without values, none of the concepts I talk about in this book will work. Without values, freedom is a dangerous concept. Freedom means that you do whatever you want as long as you're not harming others. That's one of the keys values of this book.

Another value I have is to always seek the truth. I prefer to look at life for what it is. That's who I am and that's what I believe in. It doesn't mean you should do what I do. Nor do I want to convince you of my beliefs. You should make up your own. In fact, you can do anything you want. You just have to know *what* that is. Later on, I will share how I uncovered my core values and I'll share an exercise you can do to figure out yours. Without core values we're aimless. And aimlessness is the enemy of freedom.

"When I discover who I am, I'll be free."

— Ralph Ellison

CHAPTER THREE

SACRIFICING OURSELVES

To be truly free, you have to put your own wellbeing first. But instead, we think we need to be kind, nice, and self-sacrificing. It's a naive way of looking at life. The truth is that we're afraid to be honest with others and ourselves. The truth is that you are the most important person in your life. Yes, you're more important than your kids, parents, siblings, friends, and the rest of the world. Why? Because if you're strong, all those people I just mentioned will thank you for it.

Ralph Waldo Emerson said: "The purpose of life is not to be happy. It is to be useful, to be honorable, to be compassionate, to have it make some difference that you have lived and lived well." **The ultimate way of making yourself useful is by being an accountable, responsible, strong, and stable human**

being. No one wants a weak person in their lives that always has to depend on others. No one *likes* to be weak and to be taken care of. Humans are independent and free. If we *can*, we need to rely on ourselves and pull our own weight. When we can do that, we're free. We will not look at others for answers. We figure things out on our own. That doesn't mean we're stubborn or think we know it all. We must be humble and see ourselves as a student for life. When I say we figure things out on our own, I mean that we take control. When something needs to be done, we do it or ask for help. But instead of putting our own wellbeing first, we sacrifice it for other people or things.

- When you stay in a relationship because you're afraid your partner might not be able to handle a breakup, you think you're doing the right thing, but you're making both of you weaker and you're sacrificing your own wellbeing.

- When you stay close to home so your parents won't miss you, you're sacrificing your own desires.

- When you take a job that you hate, you're sacrificing yourself for some money.

- When you stay at your job because you're too afraid to make a change, you're sacrificing a better future.

We're sacrificing ourselves all the time. We don't act in our own best interests. You know what you have to do to be free in life. You know what it takes. The answer might scare you, but that doesn't make it untrue. You still have to do it.

If you're afraid of stating your desires and wants, you're not free. And it's largely because other people often punish you for being yourself. In my relationship, I often said yes because I didn't want to disappoint my girlfriend. I thought I was being a good guy by sacrificing myself to make her happy. Man, what was I wrong. Such a thing does not exist. No one can sacrifice him or herself and feel good about it. It might take a few days, months, years, or even decades, but some day it will all come out.

"I did this for you!" Is that something a free person says? No. It's what someone says when they give in to other people's expectations. To care about other people's expectations is a sure way to end up resentful. Whether they're the expectations of your parents, partner, friend, co-workers, or society, as long as you give in, you're not free. A free person does what he or she wants. Not because people expect you to do something. The people in our lives who have high expectations of us are not to blame. They are brought up that way. They don't know any better. But you do. You want to be free of it all.

"Freedom (n.): To ask nothing. To expect nothing. To depend on nothing."

— Ayn Rand

CHAPTER FOUR

WE AVOID PAIN

So much of our time is dedicated to avoiding discomfort, pain, and suffering. We believe that's what we're supposed to do. It's a naive idea that has no foundation. When we look at life, we can't deny that it's not always fun. Every person wants to be happy and free in their own way. But avoiding pain is not the way to achieve that goal. If you truly want to become free, you must accept pain as a natural part of life.

I used to believe that was impossible. I thought we were *wired* to avoid pain. But that's false. We're wired to survive. We don't need to quote a scientist or intellectual to understand that. If we look at our actions, survival is written all over it. But it requires you to inspect your actions deeply. Why do you work? Why do you exercise? Why do you have an intimate relationship? Why do you have friends?

I thought I worked because I enjoyed work. I thought I exercised because it made me feel good. I thought I had a relationship because I loved the other person. I thought I had friends to share joy with. There's some truth in these statements. But we also have all those things in our lives because we need them to survive. How long do you think a lonely person without any skills will survive? Even though most of us like to believe we can survive on our own, the truth is we can't last a week on our own. That's not surprising. However, the problem is that we are too dependent on external factors. We fear being alone and poor. But no matter how rich you are and how many friends you have, you will still feel pain. Nothing can help you avoid it. Not your job, money in the bank, fancy gadgets, friends, a partner, parents, social media presence, status, or anything else you have in life.

When you suffer, you suffer alone. That doesn't mean all life is suffering. Somehow, people assume the ancient sages said that "life is suffering." That's not true. Suffering is a *part* of life. But in general, life is good. At least, it *can* be good. But we insist on making it shitty for ourselves by restricting ourselves. We let the fear of pain drive our decisions. That's not freedom.

When you're free from the fear of suffering, you can do what you actually want. And it turns out that what we really want requires some suffering. Think about it. Nothing worthwhile in life comes free. Sure, you can be comfortable and live your life on autopilot. But will you be happy with a life that you didn't choose? Will you feel fulfilled? Will you be free? The answer for most of us is no.

Why do we still settle for the easy life? It's because we all know that we must suffer to achieve what we want. You and I both know that all growth comes from pain. I've never met a person who achieved something great, was happy, free, or made a big breakthrough, that didn't experience pain along the way. Remember, nothing is free. You also know this. You know that comfort is a death sentence. To grow, you must do hard things. That's the purpose of life: To make yourself useful, to contribute, and feel good about what you do and who you are. And you want to do things in your *own* way.

Why are you here, reading this book? There must be some sort of pain that's driving you. Do you hate your job? Did you break up with your partner? Did you get divorced? Do your kids hate you? Do you hate yourself? Do you feel like a loser? Do you badly want to be free? Do you feel like you're wasting your life and potential? Use that pain! Welcome it. Don't avoid it. It's merely pain. On the other side, there's freedom.

"But I can't help feeling sad when something bad happens."

You don't have to laugh when a loved one passes away. That's not welcoming pain. That's running away from it. Our lives are dedicated to the avoidance of suffering. We do everything to be comfortable and to feel the least amount of pain. And that's exactly why we're not free. When you run from something, you're not free by definition. Would a free person try to avoid anything that's not life threatening? No, if you're free, you're not afraid of the invisible forces that hold us captive. That's my point. And it took me a long time to discover this complex truth about life.

When do you know you're truly free? The moment you stop running.

"Suffering becomes beautiful when anyone bears great calamities with cheerfulness, not through insensibility but through greatness of mind."

—Aristotle

CHAPTER FIVE

SOCIAL OBLIGATIONS

When you feel you're obligated to say yes to a friend, or that you have to behave a certain way around your friends, you're not free. Remember, true freedom is to do what you want and to be who you are. Can you say that when you're around your friends?

Too often, the answer is no. When your friends are disappointed that you can't join a night out because you want to work on your business, they are not accepting you for who you are. When your friends don't want to meet up at a quiet place, which you prefer, but choose to meet at a loud bar instead, they want you to fit in.

I don't believe in that type of fitting in. The chances are you and your friends have different values. Let me give you an example. A while back, one of my friends sent me and a few other guys who are in a WhatsApp group, an invitation to his birthday party. On a Thursday evening he causally said something like, "Hey guys, it's my birthday next weekend, and you're all invited. Let me know if you will be there." The next morning, one of the other guys posted something in the group about Calvin Klein boxer shorts being 50% off. Instead of responding to our friend, we simply talked about boxer shorts. This WhatsApp group consists of six guys who fool around all the time. We hardly take anything serious and joke around all the time. Also, everyone has busy lives and has their own problems to deal with. Two days later when my friend didn't get a reply from us, he told us he was disappointed we didn't respond and immediately left the group.

He wasn't interested in *why* the others didn't respond. Also, it didn't mean we were not coming. We were pretty close and had been going to each other's birthdays for years. Now, I also had my fair share of challenges that week. It's not important to go into those because I don't want to use them as an excuse. I messaged my friend to apologize for not responding. I could have let him know something, anything. But he didn't really welcome it. He was still pissed off. I don't get that. People all have their own lives and I understand that. Just because I don't reply for two days, I'm not invited to your birthday anymore? By removing himself he screwed up the whole group dynamic, and as a result, it's much quieter these days. But I don't mind that. I prefer to spend my time with people who are similar. I don't have expectations of my friends.

My best friends and I, including my brother Daniel, have never had issues for as long as we've known each other. I've also never had fights with my brother, and that's something a lot of siblings find hard to believe. I'm older, and every time I wanted to tease my brother as kids, my mother told me off: "You never, ever, fight with your brother. You support each other. You only have one brother and you don't screw that relationship up." That's why loyalty to those who are close to you is also my core value. I don't fight with people who are on the same side as me—ever. I also don't get disappointed by their actions. I trust them and I know they mean well. That's only true for the people I call family and close friends.

I've known one of my best friends, Derek, my whole life. We became friends in elementary school and have remained that way. Even though he lives in a different city, we still text regularly, and see each other a few times a year. He read all my books before they were published and gave me feedback. Never have we had an issue or a misunderstanding. The reason is that he accepts me the way I am, and I accept him the way he is.

Derek lives a simple life and has told me on numerous occasions that he is content with his life. I'm almost the opposite. I'm also content, but I'm ambitious and want to grow my business. We lead very different lives. But we're still friends. How is that? We share the same values. Remember the friend I mentioned earlier who removed himself from a WhatsApp group? I don't want to spend my time with people who get upset just because I don't respond to a message. You should at least hear what's going on. Maybe I was ill or had something serious to take care of. Bad friends are not bad people. Bad friends are simply bad friends for each other. I was a bad friend to him, and he was a bad friend to me. We live in a free world. He can do whatever he wants. And I can too. And I choose not to spend my time with him.

"But you're friends."

What's your definition of friendship? Because we might have different definitions. In the past I thought once you became friends, you had to stay that way. But people change. When you have little in common and don't really like each other, you need to move on. I can say that he and I were never real friends in the first place. Think about it. Can you really be yourself around certain friends? If not, they are not the right friends for you. Spend less time with them and spend more time with the friends who accept you for who you are.

You can't please everyone. You can't make everybody like you. This is your life and you can do what you want. If you don't want to visit people's parties or gatherings, then don't. By saying yes to everybody, we think we're avoiding their disappointment. That might be true. But you're disappointing yourself with these types of social obligations.

So much of our frustration comes from spending time with people we have little in common with. We feel obligated to visit every person who asks us. Co-workers, distant family members, family of family, friends of friends. If you *want* to spend time with them, it's a different story. In that case, you're free. But most of the time, we feel restricted by social obligations. That's not freedom.

"A true friend is someone who lets you have total freedom to be yourself – and especially to feel. Or not feel. Whatever you happen to be feeling at the moment is fine with them. That's what real love amounts to – letting a person be what he really is."

— *Jim Morrison*

CHAPTER SIX

GUILT

Since we all have the urge to be free, we sometimes act in our best interests. We think about ourselves sometimes. That's good. But why do you feel bad about it? Guilt.

Our society believes that selfishness is bad. But evolution thinks it's good. Otherwise, none of us would be here. We survive by thinking about ourselves (and our kids) first. Otherwise, we can't help others. We've established that in the previous chapter. But if you don't accept that philosophy of life you will always feel guilty. Others who have a naive and unrealistic view of life will make you feel that way.

"Why are you so selfish?!" People say this in a negative way. It's almost like a curse word. In those cases we should say,

"Why wouldn't I act according to my nature?" After all, it's not natural to be selfless. What good are you to others without a sense of self? Without having skills and capabilities? Without wisdom? Every person on earth has something to contribute. Too often, people use excuses to avoid responsibility. "But I'm useless. I can't do anything, and I have nothing." A free person never says that. Old or young, physically strong or not, capable or not—everyone has something to give. But if they neglect their own worth, they cannot.

A free person never feels guilty about decisions that make things better. A free person has strong core values and always acts according to values that are based on the common good. A free person is not a psychopath. A free person wants good for all. Hence, a free person should always act with good intentions. And good intentions do not make you feel guilty.

But when a free person screws up and becomes cynical about life, he or she *should* feel guilty. That's the only good guilt there is. When you know you are doing the wrong thing. When you're harming others with your actions. And when you squander your potential. With all those hours you're wasting on complaining, binge watching T.V. shows, playing video games, online shopping, spying on other people on social media—you could have done something useful. You could have been selfish. You could have made your life better. And as a result, other people's lives would be better too. When you do the right thing others will be inspired to do the same. When you develop yourself, you can provide value.

The free see life for what it is. To do as you want and to be what you are, you must *do* and *be* without guilt.

"A society that puts equality before freedom will get neither. A society that puts freedom before equality will get a high degree of both."

— *Milton Friedman*

CHAPTER SEVEN

PRESSURE TO BE SUCCESSFUL

We pursue goals that have nothing to do with what we want. We feel an external pressure to succeed in life. It looks something like this:

1. **Get a degree**—Not from just any university. No, you need to go to the best. The more you spend on your degrees the better.

2. **Have a job with status**—Something like a lawyer, engineer, CEO, executive, doctor, etc. And preferably, you should be the boss of something. You should have people working "underneath you."

3. **Get married**—Just a relationship is not enough. Everyone needs to get married and stayed married. Single is not good either. And being divorced is even worse.

4. **Have material wealth**—You need a new car, branded clothes, and other stuff to show off. You also need to travel every year and stay at fancy hotels.

If you experience the pressure to become successful according to any definition that's not your own, you're not free. You should never accept other people's definition of success. But the pressure to be successful in the eyes of society hovers around us constantly. It never goes away. You can push it away for a while, but it always pops up again.

There's a voice inside your mind that says, "You're not successful enough. You need to make more money. You need a bigger house. You need to be famous. You need to be more like this or that person."

From the outside, people look successful. When you look at their social media profiles or meet with them, they pretend they have it all together. They talk about their vacations to Greece or Cancun. They post pictures of themselves and write pretentious captions that make them look wise or spiritual. They try hard to appear happy and free.

But a free person does not want to appear free. You simply want to *be* free. There's no need to show off. In fact, people who try too hard are not trying to impress *you*. They also don't want to be better than *you*. That's not what social media or bragging is about. No, they are trying to convince *themselves*. The wise quotes they post on their Instagram are directed towards themselves. They don't want to show you they are doing well. They want to trick themselves into believing they are happy and free. But deep down, they are the opposite. They are restricted by obligations. The house, the car, the vacations, the fancy clothes—it all has a price. And at night, they can't sleep because the pressure to keep up feels like a bowling ball on their chest.

That's the pressure to be successful. And you need to remove that pressure to be free. **You are only successful if you're free to live your life the way you want.** *What* you do is up to you. And there's no pressure to do anything.

Imaginary Deadlines

We all have imaginary deadlines in our head. We think we need to earn certain amounts of money before we're 30 or 40 or 50. We need to get married after two, three or five years of being together. We need to switch jobs after three years. We need to be c-level executives before age 40. We need to publish our first book before 35. Our business needs to generate seven figures within three years.

What deadlines you are trapped by? If you think you're in a hurry, you make different decisions. Do you recognize that feeling of having lunch or dinner, knowing you have an appointment in thirty minutes? Let's say you're having lunch with a friend and it's 12PM. You have an appointment with someone at 2PM. You'll start feeling uneasy after an hour—

especially if the food hasn't arrived. You're thinking to your-self, "So if I leave at 1:30PM, I should be on time. But what if there's traffic? I might need to leave early. But I'm having a good time!" We live our whole lives in that state of mind. We're trapped by thoughts of what we should do next. We're always a step ahead of ourselves. We're going through all the alternatives in our head. But in this case, all the alternatives are bad.

The pressure to succeed forces us to live in the future. We're trapped in a future that hasn't arrived yet. And as a result, we miss the present. A present that's fully at our disposal. We can do anything we want with this moment. But we don't use that power.

"The only way to deal with an unfree world is to become so ab-solutely free that your very existence is an act of rebellion."

— Albert Camus

CHAPTER EIGHT

FOLLOWING OUR EMO-TIONS

We believe every thought and feeling that pops up in our minds. Who ever said our thoughts are telling the truth? We're trapped by our thoughts and emotions when we lose control over ourselves. When you always follow your emotions and random thoughts, you're not free to follow what you really want. Sadness, anger, overwhelm, confusion, stress—all emotions that hold us captive. Emotional freedom means you're free from all the emotions that make you unfree.

A free person still has emotions like everyone else. But while everyone else is stuck in repetitive thought patterns, the free person is never idle. A free person moves on. A free person doesn't give weight to their emotions. The free person merely observes and doesn't judge. A free person also doesn't follow through on every single thought and emotion.

To be emotionally free, you're always in the moment, experiencing whatever is in front of you. Sometimes you enjoy yourself, and sometimes you don't. That's how life works. It's not always fun and games. Sometimes things get rough. But still, a free person doesn't let their emotions make them go crazy. I used to let my thoughts go wild. I followed through on every single thought and emotion I had.

When my girlfriend and I broke up I felt sad. During the first week I lost all my motivation. I thought I would spend my life with her and had even thought about marriage. But I was trapped. Not only inside the relationship itself, but also when it ended. My thoughts and emotions told me different things. One minute I confirmed to myself that we weren't compatible and wanted different things from life. The next minute I tried to convince myself that I made the wrong decision and we should give it another try. But this wasn't the first time we had issues. We had already tried to save the relationship and knew it wouldn't work out. Instead of following through, I started observing my emotions. I realized that nearly everything that popped up in my mind was false. The emotions tried to keep me busy.

Emotions have nothing else to do but hold you captive. But at some point, I realized I am not my thoughts. I have the desire to be free, content, and joyful—even during tough times.

That's who I am. I am not the chaos that my thoughts want to create. I am here, in the moment. When I have a thought or an urge, I can distance myself from that thought. I play mind games with myself all the time. If my mind tells me, "Get to the gym" I sometimes don't listen. Even though I know that working out is good for me and I try to get daily exercise, I also realize that I'm free to do whatever I want. If I let my habits and thoughts take control, I'm no longer the person who's calling the shots. "But why would you not go to the gym if it's good for you?" It's counterintuitive, I know. But this exercise is all about being free from your thoughts, urges, and desires. You want to *decide* to do something. You don't want your emotions to dictate your actions.

A lot of intellectuals and scientists don't believe that we have ultimate control over our actions. They are right. We're influenced by millions of factors and free will is probably only an illusion. But that doesn't mean we can't try to transcend that idea. Normal people follow their emotions all the time. When we feel tired despite having slept 8 hours, we give in to our emotions that say we're tired. "I'm tired today" is what we say to ourselves and give up our day like it's worthless. Have you ever done that? Until recently, I did that all the time. I just thought there was no way I could save that day. After all, I was tired and grouchy. I assumed there would be another day. But who can guarantee you a new day? That's the true illusion.

Our emotions remain complex and no one knows exactly how they work. We can only try to understand ourselves. That's why we need to observe ourselves more. It will not only increase our awareness; it will set us free from clinging to our emotions.

"Nobody can bring you peace but yourself."

—*Ralph Waldo Emerson*

CHAPTER NINE

LACK OF SELF-ESTEEM

Sometimes, the problem is not that we let our thoughts or other people hold us back. Sometimes, we feel the urge to be free and want to act on it, but when we try to break free and do our own thing, we *can't*. We don't believe in ourselves.

You can do all the right things but still be unfree to pursue your true desires. A free person doesn't have limitations. When you're free, you go after what you desire. You actually do what you want.

Being free is not saying, "I can do what I want" and then sitting at home doing nothing. I fell into that trap too. At one point I was emotionally free, didn't care about other people's expectations, and also made good money—but I didn't act enough on my desires. For example, I wanted to invest my money more but was scared to lose it. I lacked self-esteem. I didn't believe enough in my ability to make good investment decisions.

I wasn't free because I desired something but didn't act on it. I wanted to invest because I enjoyed it and wanted to build wealth. But if you never pull the trigger because you're afraid or lack self-esteem, you're still trapped. It's different if you don't invest because you decided to pass on a specific investment for a certain reason.

Or if you're still saving your money. That's different. I had the opportunity to invest in a property but hesitated too long. I pretended I wasn't sure about the property. But in reality, I wasn't sure about myself.

To be free is to do what you want. It's not something you say just to sound rebellious. Everyone can *say* they are free. But are they really free? Freedom is not about impressing others. You live for yourself and no one cares about your freedom but you. When a lack of self-esteem holds us captive, we feel we can't do what we want. We play it safe. We appear free, but from the inside, we're not truly free. In the back of our minds, we always feel something is holding us back. But self-esteem is not just about believing in yourself.

I realized that I needed to learn more about investing. I read more books and I regularly met up with a good friend who has a large property portfolio. When knowledge increased, my self-esteem did too. And once you *do* what you desire, you're free.

"This is the highest wisdom that I own; freedom and life are earned by those alone who conquer them each day anew."

—*Johann Wolfgang von Goeth*

e

CHAPTER TEN

SHORT-TERM HAPPINESS

We all have desires. The strongest are being free, independent, and happy. Happiness has a direct impact on the quality of our lives. Everything is better when you're happy. But why is that? Is life better because you're happy? Or are you happy because your life good? It's both.

Happiness is a feeling that comes and goes. No one is happy 24/7. But there are people who are systematically unhappy. There are also people who always find reasons to be happy. No matter what your natural tendency is, it's impossible to be happy all the time. It depends on your actions. If you keep pursuing things that bring you short-term happiness, you relapse and often feel unhappy. At such moments, you can't just say, "I will be happy from now on." When positive psychology people say that happiness is a choice, skeptical people say that it's not that simple. The skeptics say that you can't just decide to be happy if your life is bad. I agree with both.

To be happy, you need to decide to *do* things that give you inner happiness. When we chase pleasure, we might feel short-term happiness, but it's not the same as the inner satisfaction I'm talking about. A free person does things that give him *lasting* happiness. That's the trick. Set yourself free from the excessive desire for things that only make you happy for a short period. Instead, create a life that's full of activities and things that bring you lasting happiness.

What you'll find is that lasting happiness is either free or doesn't cost much. You don't need to spend $50K on a wedding to enjoy it. You don't need to travel to the other side of the world to rest. You don't need to have a Rolex to check the time. You don't need a Range Rover to drive around town.

It doesn't mean you shouldn't do those things if you're already wealthy. If a free person could choose between wealth and poverty, he or she will choose wealth. But you're not afraid of poverty. If it comes, it comes. **You will always find ways to be happy.** When you're free from worry, stress, and negative emotions, you will have enough energy to improve your life anyway. That's why free people are often wealthy too. In contrast, unhappy and unfree people are struggling to make ends meet. They are stuck in negative emotions and they settle for less. They don't believe that they can become free. In that case, they need to commit to improvement. Sure, you won't be instantly happy. Nothing that's worth it in life happens instantly. To live freely and do what you want, you need to pay the price. You need to be optimistic and never settle for anything less than total freedom.

But no matter how much wealth you have, acquiring more just for the sake of *having* more is something that unfree people do. That's because you can't be truly happy by acquiring things. Ask some of the richest people in the world. They have money, but they are not free. Their excessive desire makes them chase short-term happiness and pleasure. It's easy to get trapped on the hedonic treadmill. That's when you keep on satisfying your desires. But the effect doesn't last. That's what I call short-term happiness. Avoid it.

"Freedom is not procured by a full enjoyment of what is desired, but by controlling the desire."

— *Epictetus*

CHAPTER ELEVEN

LACK OF VISION

When you're caged by the mundanities of daily life, you're not free. You'll feel like that movie *Groundhog Day*. Every day looks the same and you seem to go nowhere. No goal. No vision. You're trapped inside your own life.

That's how unfree most of us are. For me, this was the worst feeling in the world. It is for that reason that I drastically changed my life four years ago. At some point I felt I was repeating the same things, year in, year out. Monday through Friday, work. Go to the gym three times a week. Buy groceries on Saturday morning, and do something "fun" the rest of the day and evening. Go shopping, eat at a nice restaurant, go see a movie. Then, rest on Sunday so you can repeat the cycle on Monday. And there are also activities most of us repeat yearly.

The yearly summer vacation or the winter ski trip. By 2015, I had been doing those things for nearly 5 years after I graduated. I looked at my past, and then I extrapolated it.

I realized that if I kept doing what I had been doing I would get the same results every single year. At the time I had a relationship. The next step was probably to get married and try to have kids. Did I really want to live my life that way? Without any vision for the future? Without any real goals? Sure, I had superficial goals like, "Get a promotion, earn six figures, buy a Mercedes." And some other meaningless goals. But I didn't have a *vision*.

What did I want to accomplish in life? What's my life about? What matters? How can I make a contribution? I didn't have all the answers then, but now I realize that I desperately wanted to be free. At that time I was far from free. I was trapped inside all the things I wrote about in the previous chapters. I strongly felt the desire to be free. I couldn't stand the idea of spending my life the way I had been doing until I died. What a waste. I'm not saying any of the things I mentioned are bad. *I* simply didn't want that for my life. I wanted the freedom to live my life the way I wanted.

But instead, I was trapped inside my own head. Sometimes you want to blame others for your frustration. "I'm not free because of my partner and family." I've used that excuse too. It might be true that you're unfree right now. But it's not because of other people unless they are literally holding you captive. If that's the case, you need to kick them in the ass and seek help. But if you're not physically restrained by anyone, you're unfree because of your *own* decisions. Your decisions led you to where you are.

"The most important kind of freedom is to be what you really are. You trade in your reality for a role. You trade in your sense for an act. You give up your ability to feel, and in exchange, put on a mask. There can't be any large-scale revolution until there's a personal revolution, on an individual level. It's got to happen inside first."

— Jim Morrison

CHAPTER TWELVE

THE RULER OF YOUR OWN KINGDOM

You, my friend, are the ruler of your kingdom. You got yourself where you are. And you will get yourself to where you want to be.

The keyword is responsibility. Four years ago I took responsibility for my own life. I realized that if I wanted to be free, *I* needed to make it happen. No one else will do it for you. Not your parents, brother, sister, partner, or friend. No one but you is responsible for your life. **Everything you do must be a decision.**

You work because you decided to have that career. You have a relationship or marriage with the person *you* chose. You spend time with people because you decided to. Everything should also be true the other way around. Your co-workers or clients should only work with you because they want to work with a person like you. Your spouse should want to be with you because you're a good person. You need to be the type of person your spouse would want. And that's also true for your friends. They are also the rulers of their own kingdoms. No one forces them to do something. Everything they do is because they decided to. **A free person respects another person's freedom more than anything else in the world. Why? Because freedom *is* the most important thing.**

Your parents, partner, manager, co-workers, and friends are not your boss. You are not anyone else's boss either. You are only your own boss. Everything you do in life is your choice. Even in the bleakest circumstances, you decide to endure it. You never surrender your power to someone else. You protect your own kingdom with your life. Never, ever, will you give up your sovereignty.

However, you *will* give up everything else that's required so you can *keep* that absolute power. What are those things?

In Part II, I share the things I've given up. It was not easy and it's a continuous battle. I had to give up many things in order to be free. But remember, freedom is the highest aim in life. There's nothing greater or nobler than freedom. That means everything you give up has less worth than freedom. And only a stupid person trades something of value for something that's worth less. Keep that in the back of your mind as you read Part II. Yes, some things are hard to give up. But in return, you will get something that has a high value: Freedom.

"Freedom makes a huge requirement of every human being. With freedom comes responsibility. For the person who is unwilling to grow up, the person who does not want to carry his own weight, this is a frightening prospect."

— *Eleanor Roosevelt*

PART II

THE PRICE

"You wanna fly, you got to give up the shit that weighs you down."

— Toni Morrison

CHAPTER THIRTEEN

CERTAINTY

Why do you seek freedom? Do you never want to worry about money? Do you want to have a little peace? No more stress? Finally certainty about the future, right?

I used to want those things. But that's not freedom. No matter how much money you have or how self-confident you are, life always remains uncertain. Deep down, we all know we're a fragile species. We know we can die in an accident tomorrow. It doesn't require much force either. An unlucky fall is enough to end your life. That's not the only thing that can end us. Viruses and bacteria kill people as well. That's merely our *physical* fragility. Our careers are also fragile. Jobs disappear, highly sought-after skills change, industries change, and economies collapse.

Life is change. Nothing in our power can change the nature of life. To find true freedom in life, we must accept that life is unstable. We have to give up our drive for safety, stability, and certainty. This idea has existed for centuries, but if this is the first time you've heard it you will resist giving up certainty. You will say, "But what about..."

Think about it. When during the course of history did the world stay the same for a long period of time? Can you name a country, company, or organization that has never changed since inception? How about yourself? Even though we can stall as adults, the first 18 years of our lives is nothing but change. And you can argue that people in their twenties still change until they settle into a career. You see? Life *is* change. A free person doesn't resist that. A free person welcomes uncertainty. That will not only make you free, it will also make you less susceptible to the things an unfree person fears.

Losing people, your job, money, strength—most of us fear loss. We think we can reach a point in life where things will be stable. Where we don't lose anything. That day never comes. As long as we live, we have to deal with change. **Adapting to change is real freedom.** That's why the first thing I did four years ago was to give up certainty.

Often, we look to *others* to give us certainty. I regularly see people celebrating when they receive a permanent contract from an employer. We expect that the company will take care of our future. We think we're "set." But instead, we become more vulnerable to change. When you work for decades at one company and only learn how to do one thing, you risk becoming obsolete. Companies and economies change. There's a high probability your job will disappear in time. When that happens, where's the certainty you thought you had? You don't have any other income streams. And you didn't learn skills that you can apply somewhere else. You see, assuming that you're set for life is true uncertainty.

Whether we like it or not, no one has the tools or information to completely remove uncertainty. We assume that experts have the answers to everything we need to deal with. Philosophers don't know everything about life. Doctors don't know everything about the human body. Business consultants don't know everything about running companies. Financial advisors don't know everything about markets. If they did, they could predict the future. We laugh at people who say they are psychic or clairvoyant, but we don't laugh at people who make predictions about the stock market. In effect, it's the same thing. Predicting the stock market might require more information, but you can't predict most things in life with 100% certainty. We all know we will die, have to pay taxes, and that certain bad habits lead to our destruction. Those things are obvious. So why do we still try to remove uncertainty by looking to others for answers?

We haven't come to terms with uncertainty yet. At some point, I hope it's now, you need to accept that life is uncertain. Anything can happen. Are you comfortable with that? You're only comfortable with that when you stop worrying about the future. I used to worry a lot. What happens if I lose my money? What if my business goes bust? What if the people I love die? What if I get ill?

Today, I realize that anything can happen and that I have to deal with it. We don't control much in life. However, we do control our personal freedom. You decide how you look at the world. And accepting uncertainty is entirely within your control.

Giving up certainty doesn't mean giving up responsibility. It doesn't mean you should blow your money fast. It doesn't give you permission to be an asshole. It also doesn't mean you should shut down your emotions. No one says you should laugh when someone dies. We're still human and we have emotions. Grabbing a bottle of Jack Daniels, hooking up with a stranger, snorting coke, binge watching T.V. shows, eating 5000 calories a day—we do those things to numb the pain that uncertainty brings. You can't deal with uncertainty. And you think you will find certainty in those things. But we all know that's not the path to happiness and freedom.

"Freedom means doing what you want... And I want to down a bottle of the best whiskey."

That's what the cynics tell me when I talk about freedom. I get it. It's another way of hiding. Instead of taking responsibility, they try to make fun of freedom. I'm all about having fun. But is getting drunk, screwing up your life, being addicted, and destroying your body fun? C'mon. Everybody can do whatever they want, and I don't try to force my way of living on people. But don't tell me it's "good" to screw up yourself. There's nothing noble about self-destruction. It's downright sad. People who glorify self-destruction should grow up and face the uncertain nature of life. Just because we don't know what will happen tomorrow doesn't mean we should throw away today.

Freedom means that we accept anything that happens. Give up certainty and be free as a reward. It's not easy, but we've already established that freedom is worth it. That's why we should never complain about the price. We should only focus on the reward. Would you rather pay a high price for something? Or not be able to buy it at all?

"Most people do not really want freedom, because freedom involves responsibility, and most people are frightened of responsibility."

—Sigmund Freud

CHAPTER FOURTEEN

COMFORT

This is counterintuitive at first because so much of our life is dedicated to avoiding discomfort. I'm saying that you should flip it. Instead of seeking comfort, seek discomfort. When you accept uncertainty, you will find some freedom. But if you want total freedom, you must take it one step further. **Merely accepting uncertainty is not enough, we have to strengthen ourselves by giving up comfort too.**

On top of that, comfort is useless. It doesn't serve a purpose. On the contrary, when you do uncomfortable things, you will grow. We all know that the only way to become strong is to do hard things and endure suffering. You become physically stronger by putting stress on your body. You become mentally and emotionally stronger by enduring hurt, sadness, grief, and loneliness.

But instead of seeking those things, I used to avoid them. I didn't train my body to become stronger. And I did everything to avoid emotional pain. Death, grief, sadness, bullying, fear of the unknown, illness, injury, being broke, losing friends, being alone, breaking up, and physical pain were the main things I tried to avoid. We don't want to suffer through things that make us feel bad. Why? The reason we're in pain is that we fear suffering. When you welcome it, you will find that suffering is merely suffering. It will not break you. In fact, it will make you stronger.

If you commit yourself to growth and to improving your life, career, business, and relationships, you're going to suffer. Nothing comes free. And nothing can grow without pain. That's exactly the reason I chose to do nothing for years instead of chasing my desire to become free. I wanted to avoid pain and be comfortable. But what I didn't realize is that doing nothing is actually worse. When you don't grow, you decay. There's no such thing as protecting the status quo.

As you're reading this, cells in your body are dying. That's because of entropy. The natural direction of life is downwards—towards disorder. Your relationship will die if you don't invest time, love, and energy in it. It's the same for your career, business, and job. There's someone else, right now, ready to take your spot. That's not bad. It's good for all of us. It simply means that you *must* grow. The other option is to crumble. To be free is to accept the nature of life. You need to work with the laws of nature. You can't go against them and try to change things that can't be changed. That's not freedom. That's foolishness.

When I finally committed to growth in 2015, I was willing to pay the price on each front. I quit my job and left London, the city I loved living in. I realized that I was unfree. I wasn't passionate about my job and I couldn't be myself. I gave up everything and moved back in with my parents. I had about $15K in savings, and that was about it.

But I fully committed to making a living as a writer. For the first two years I worked all day, every day. I also worked on my family business that we started in 2010. Other than working, I committed to exercising every day. And I also wanted to become more mindful in my relationships. I wanted to grow spiritually, financially, mentally, physically, emotionally—on every level.

Basically, I wanted to get my shit together. And every day was painful. I failed a lot. I'm still like that. Growth hurts whether you are a beginner or pro. And there's nothing you can do about it to make it easier. You simply have to commit and go *through* the pain. Because on the other side, you will find freedom.

When you set out on a new path in life, you need to say goodbye to your old one. And that may be the hardest part. You have to say goodbye to your old habits, thinking patterns, and maybe to your job, business, or even people in your life. Freedom means living the way you want. And by now, you know what stands in the way of achieving freedom. What's limiting your freedom? Is it your job? Family? Partner? Friends? Or is it you? At some point you'll have to decide *what* is holding you back and then bring closure to whatever it is. You must identify what it is and then consciously choose a new life direction. And accept that without suffering there is no growth.

Achieving anything worthwhile in life is difficult. There will be a lot of suffering that comes from failure, disappointment, and pushing your limits. But remember, life *itself* is not suffering. Some people believe that The Buddha once said that. If you do some research on Google, you will find that it's one of those classic misquotations.

The Buddha never said that. Suffering is *a part* of life. But that doesn't mean that your whole life is suffering. No, life is great when you're free. You do what you want and spend time with people you like. That's what we're after. And if I have to suffer to get there, I will go through it with a smile on my face. That's the distinction. You suffer on your own terms. You use the pain from suffering to make a change.

No matter what we do, suffering will always remain a part of life. If we remain caged in our free world, we suffer because we're not pursuing our urge to be free. You see? We can't escape it. So why not *use* suffering to become stronger? When we experience hard times, we grow. And when we keep growing every day, we will simultaneously become better at dealing with the challenges of life. When we finally believe and *know* we can overcome any challenge that life throws at us, we're free.

"Be patient and tough; someday this pain will be useful to you."

— Ovid

CHAPTER FIFTEEN

LIES

We lie so much it becomes a habit. We don't even know we're lying so much. Not only do we lie to others when we say we have a doctor's appointment to get out of something, but we also lie to ourselves when we deny our desires. "I'm fine." No, you're not. Be honest about that.

When you lie, you live in deception. To be free, you need to give it up. Tell the truth and see everything for what it is. The truth will only make you stronger. Too often, we hide from reality. We don't want to face our problems. But our problems are not problems. It is merely the truth. How can the truth be a problem?

Telling the truth means seeing things for what they are. It

means being honest with your emotions. It means not hiding from reality.

Remember, being free means to live as you are. **You don't have to lie about who you are, what you like, and what you do. Just be yourself.** That is very easy to say but hard to do. It requires giving up lies. For me, it meant that I stopped trying to be someone I'm not. I am a guy who likes to read, write, watch movies, and have deep conversations with interesting people. If I don't want to do something, I don't do it. And I take full responsibility for it. That doesn't mean I stay in bed all day. That's something I don't want. Some people find that hard to believe. I hate laziness. I can't be around people who are lazy. Why? Because I used to be that way and I can't stand the idea of being like that again. That's the truth. I'm not perfect. But it is what it is. It's better to accept who you are.

It also means accepting your emotions. If you're sad, don't pretend you're happy. Affirmations and positive psychology don't work when shit hits the fan. Honesty is the only long-term strategy. The truth is that life changes all the time. Good times follow bad times, and vice versa. Go with it. Don't resist. And be honest about how you feel.

Being honest also means you should let others know who you are. Too often, we hide our personality from others. We think they will judge us and stop liking us. Who gives a shit? If they don't like you, screw them. There are enough people who *will* like you.

The thing is, good and genuine people don't like fake people. That's how a lot of us get stuck in a vicious cycle. You hide your real personality from people, you struggle internally, you seem faceless, and people who *want* to get to know you, *can't*. As a result, you push good people away because you're not being genuine. Trying to be someone else is a recipe for disaster. I've learned to be honest with people about who I am and what I like. Of course, you need to know who you are. But communication will bring you a long way. Talk about the things you like and don't like about life with others. That will help you to understand yourself.

"But what if people react a certain way? What if I don't fit in?" If you think like that, freedom is not for you. A free person doesn't have those thoughts. When you're free, you do what you want. People can and will judge you all the time. But it should have no impact on you. Simply brush off any disturbance like that and move on.

Some people have a hard time with this way of looking at life because it seems harsh. But they can't say that it doesn't work. It might be difficult at first, because so many of us are caged by social restrictions. We think we need to be polite and not offend others. You can still be that way. Just say you don't like something in a polite way. Who cares? Just don't bully or harm people. Other than that, do what you like.

Do you know why I gave up lies? Because every time you tell a lie, it eats up a bit of you from the inside. It eats your character. If you keep telling enough lies, you become a characterless person. A no one. For example, let's say your partner asks you whether you want to go on a vacation this summer. You immediately think: "If I say no, she will be disappointed. She will be sad, and I have to live with her. But the truth is that we're low on cash this summer because we have to re-do the bathroom. I don't think it's responsible to spend two grand on a vacation. But if I say that, she won't like it." And before you know it, you say this: "Sure, honey! Let's go on a vacation!" The pattern repeats itself in our career as well. Our boss or co-worker asks us for a favor, and we say yes because we're afraid to tell the truth that we're spread too thin and can't take on extra work. If you run a business or are a freelancer, it's exactly the same. You see an opportunity, know that now is not the right time, and you lie to yourself: Let's go for it! LIES!

Be honest with yourself and others, my friend. It hurts for a second, but your life will be so much better. Like we talked about in the previous chapters, a free person is not afraid to suffer. If the price of being honest is judgment or sadness, so be it. You'll still be free. That's the real prize.

"The truth will set you free, but first it will make you miserable."

— *James A. Garfield*

CHAPTER SIXTEEN

INCOMPATIBLE PEOPLE

Nobody can thrive on their own. You're better with good people around you. The problem is that most of us surround ourselves with incompatible people. And we keep those people in our lives because we're afraid to be alone. That's the opposite of being free. The free person spends time with people who share the same values. There are millions of people on earth. Seek the ones who are like you. And say goodbye to people who are not like you. Does your partner want to complain and be negative? You will be a prisoner of their emotional energy. Don't be afraid to be alone. It's better than being close to people who drain all your energy. The reality is that we can't change people. It's better to accept that.

Instead of fighting with people who are not compatible with

you, seek people who share the same values as you. Other people who also value freedom never expect you to be someone you're not.

Incompatible Friends

You know that you have incompatible friends when your friends frustrate you. If you're always on time and very orderly, and one of your friends is the opposite, it will be difficult to do things together. If you prefer quiet time with your friend and he/she likes to go to a bar, one of you will have a bad time.

Friendship is not about sacrifice. It's about having a good time together. And there are many people you can have a good time with. There are also a lot of people you simply can't connect with. No need to force it. No one says you *have* to be friends with your co-workers, neighbors, or fellow students. You can be polite and friendly with them. But you don't need to go to their parties or spend time with them if you don't want to. You can do anything you want. If you *want* to spend time with people, then do it. If not, then don't.

Incompatible Partner

It gets more complicated with our romantic relationships. My ex-girlfriend and I were not compatible. Despite that, we even talked about marriage. How did we get that far? Love is complicated and I don't have the answers, but I do know that love should be free of expectations. And where do expectations come from? They come from the desire for our partner to *behave* or *be* a certain way. It comes from incompatibility. Love means accepting people for who they are. That's something almost everyone agrees with. But it's hard if you are in a relationship with someone who has different values than you.

You might have things in common, but if you don't share the same core values, you will not understand each other on a deep level. Every time you think to yourself, "Why do you do this or that?" It's a sign you're incompatible. When two people understand each other, they don't ask *why* in a defensive way. I'm not talking about asking why out of curiosity.

You should never defend who you are and what you do. When people say, "Why did you do that!" They are judging. They are saying, "You shouldn't have done that, you should have done something I approve of." That's not freedom. It's emotional captivity. You're not free to be yourself. But here's the thing: You ARE free to do what you want and be as you are. In fact, you need to be free.

If you've been in a relationship with someone who's incompatible, you know what I'm talking about. Or maybe you're in one now. You know, I've read many books on relationships, talked to happily married couples, and talked a lot with my girlfriends in the past.

We had a lot of things in common. We had the same sense of humor, liked the same movies, enjoyed taking long walks together, both came from close-knit families. Nonetheless, there were too many things we didn't understand about each other to be compatible. That's why I decided to end those relationships. I'd rather be alone than with someone I'm not a match with.

This goes both ways; I don't wish incompatibility on my partner either. She should be with someone who shares the same values. It's not a matter of good or bad. I don't want to judge people. If you want to live your life a certain way, who am I to say something about it? On a personal level, I prefer to spend my time with people who do get me. And trust me, there are a lot of people who get you.

You just have to open yourself up to others. "But what about opening yourself up to other ways of thinking?" I'm a proponent of that in any other setting. I read books about different philosophies and try to learn about people who are different from me. I also like to receive feedback from people don't agree with me. But when it comes to my private life, I like to be with people who share the same values. That doesn't mean I surround myself with "yes men" in my career.

"Him that I love, I wish to be free – even from me."

— *Anne Morrow Linbergh*

Loneliness Is Temporarily

If you think *no one* gets you, the problem is not other people, it's you. Don't use freedom as an excuse to judge people or become resentful. We're social animals and are meant to live with others. We shouldn't suffer unnecessarily just because of incompatibility. When people stay in relationships with people that have different values (romantically or friendly), they are afraid of the truth. They haven't given up lies and stability yet. They choose to lie to themselves and be comfortable.

"Better to spend time with people who don't get me than to be alone." That's the mindset of an unfree person. Why is being alone so bad? It's often only temporarily. It doesn't mean you should lock yourself up. It's the same when you say goodbye to incompatible friends. If you're an energetic, positive, and fun person who's free, you will attract others. The most important thing is that you're genuine. Don't be ashamed of who you are.

Be honest about what you like and the things you enjoy. Just put yourself in a place where other people are; go to places where people are who share the same values. And don't judge—seek out people from all walks of life. You're only looking for common values—not people who speak the same language, are the same sex, or *look* like you. That's too superficial. Also, it's discrimination and prejudice. That has nothing to do with freedom.

What I mean is this: If you like books, sign up for a book club. If you like yoga, go to a yoga school. If you like running, join a running club. You have to put in some effort. And don't force anything. Only spend time with people who you're naturally attracted to. You don't *need* people. Both of you spend time with each other because you *want* to. That's real freedom to be as you are.

"I wish that every human life might be pure transparent freedom."

— *Simone de Beauvoir*

CHAPTER SEVENTEEN

FEARING MONEY

"Money makes the world go round," people say. It's true. You can't do much without money. But we fear that we will run out of money. That fear is completely unnecessary.

To get over your fear of being without money you need a plan (we will cover that in Part III). It's a process that takes time. No one becomes financially free within one or two years. However, you can change your mind set about money relatively quickly.

Don't let the fear of not having money affect important life decisions. "But I have bills to pay and mouths to feed." Stop thinking about the "buts" for a minute. That's the unfree mind trying to keep you caged. Remember, being free means doing what you want and being as you are.

Money is a resource that doesn't run out. Central banks keep printing money. And we need it to exchange resources. No one in modern civilization is self-sufficient. We need each other to survive and thrive. That's the system of living we agreed on centuries ago. Some people try to fight it and disagree with it. Everyone is free to do what they want, but you don't have to agree with the system to be free. This is simply how humans exchange goods and services that we *need*. And since the system has been around for centuries, one could safely assume it works. If there were better alternatives, people would go for them. But there's no alternative to money. I don't believe that free humans voluntarily pick something that makes them worse. We're wired for survival and always pick the best viable option for everything.

How do you make sure you can always acquire money? By acquiring skills that produce money. The economy is nothing but a marketplace. People exchange time, skills, and solutions for money. If someone owns a house, he can rent it to someone who needs shelter. If someone knows how to build a bed, she can sell it to someone who wants a bed. Remember, humans are not only driven to fulfill their basic needs. If that were the case, we would only have farmers, brick layers, and carpenters in the world. Obviously, that's an oversimplification. The point is, people also have *wants*. The truth is that no one needs a new iPhone every year. But millions of people want it. And a lot of those people will probably *buy* a new iPhone every year too. That's because most of us act on our desires.

To be free is to understand human nature. When we're frustrated with the world, it comes from our lack of understanding of mankind. Isn't it better to embrace our imperfect nature? We can't help ourselves. I wish we had a perfect society, but that's not reality. However, that doesn't mean things will stay the way they are forever. We've improved many things about life. And you and I can make life better by making a contribution. We can be more rational and desire less crap. We can think about our future more. Just because humans have behaved a certain way, it doesn't mean we're doomed. We can change if we want.

The point is that money is an abundant resource. Change the way you look at it. I know that's hard if you're trying to make ends meet. But you're not doing this for me. When people criticize this idea and say superficial things like, "I decided to become a billionaire. I opened my eyes and I was still broke." I don't respond. You don't have to tell me that. This is your life and if you want to fear money, I don't judge.

Changing your mindset will help *yourself.* For years, I didn't understand how people acquired money. I thought it was finite. But that's not the case. You shouldn't be concerned with the economy or financial markets. Instead, the best thing you can do is to acquire skills that you can exchange for money. That's a much better use of your time than to be cynical and judge people who are making money.

Income Producing Skills

Before modern civilization, humans had to hunt to survive. We had to work for our food and shelter. Vacations and sick days didn't exist. You couldn't hang out at your house and play video games; you either contributed or you died.

Today, we assume we can survive without working for it. We don't need to hunt anymore, but we require other skills to build a life. The good thing is that life is much richer and we're doing things that no human could foresee centuries ago. We have the ability to be free. That didn't exist until a few hundred years. Life is easier than ever. And we have more free time than ever. But it doesn't come for free.

You need to make yourself *useful* to be free. The reason I'm not afraid of money is because I have something better: Skills. You need to acquire skills that are considered valuable in today's economy. Here are some skills I think are valuable:

- Persuasion
- Web design
- Programming
- Copywriting
- Personal productivity
- Accounting

- Project management
- Leadership
- Marketing
- Sales
- Public speaking
- Teaching

You don't have to master all these skills. Acquire at least 5 of these skills and become better at them than average people. That requires a lot of time and energy. But trust me, it's more than worth it. I'd rather read about leadership on a Saturday evening than go to a bar. I'd rather write on my free evenings than watch T.V. I'm giving up some comfort, but in return, I become more adaptable to the future with every skill I acquire or improve.

In a way, you become less susceptible to uncertainty. But all this doesn't mean I'm safe. **You can never be 100% secure in life, but if you build a solid skillset, you will always find a way to adapt.** And that's always been mankind's biggest source of success. It's not the "strong" who survive, it's those who are the most adaptable.

Having Nothing Is Better Than Being Unfree

As you become more successful in life, you acquire more wealth and possessions. You can get attached to those things.

Does that sound like freedom? Ask a rich person who is addicted to acquiring more money and can't stand losing money. That's a fearful person.

No matter what, your freedom is the most important thing. If you have to give up opportunities, potential wealth, and money, isn't that worth the price? The common mistake successful people make is to take on more work and responsibility. That can be good. But are you free?

If you're not afraid of losing it all, you are. That's why I'm always delighted to hear people answer, "I will earn it all back" when they are asked, "What will you do if you lose everything?" That's the mindset of a free person. You are not defined by your possessions or how much you're worth. You are your character. **Money only solves your *money* problems. It changes nothing about your character or who you are.**

If I have to give up my wealth for my character, I will do it in a blink of an eye. Character is the only true thing you and I have. Everything else is borrowed.

"Real freedom is having nothing. I was freer when I didn't have a cent."

—*Mike Tyson*

CHAPTER EIGHTEEN

MINDLESS ENTERTAIN-MENT

For most of my life I fulfilled my obligations and then looked for ways to be distracted or entertained. Life can be very boring with all our free time. When I was in school, I went to class and studied. And I dedicated the rest of my time to entertainment. After I got my degrees, I worked from 9 to 5 and also dedicated my free time to entertainment. I was always looking for things to do with my time. "What shall I do this weekend?" One hundred percent of my free time was spent on keeping busy.

Don't get me wrong. I still like entertainment and relaxation. But we need to give up the drive for *mindless* entertainment.

You don't have to do something "fun" every single free minute you have. That's too forced. And when you force things, you're not free. **Entertainment and pleasure are cheap; everyone can be entertained and have pleasure. In contrast, freedom is expensive. Not everyone can pay, or is willing to pay, the price.**

If you want to challenge yourself, become stronger, learn new skills, and become a better person, you must put in the time. So if you're committed to freedom, you need to give up mindless entertainment. You need to find a way to relax in a meaningful way. My favorite way of relaxing is to read, watch inspirational movies, T.V. shows, or have deep conversations with good friends. When I spend time with people I like, I don't mind what we do. Just being around good people makes you feel better. Squandering your time makes you feel bad. It's exactly like overeating or getting drunk. You feel like shit the next day. That's a waste of life. When you work on yourself and your freedom, no matter how hard it is, you will feel good. That type of work gives you pleasure. When I was in college, I wasted a lot of time on mindless entertainment and parties. But I'm glad that I always committed to studying. When I had exams, I studied hard. But it wasn't until four years ago that I really flipped the switch. I stopped all the mindless entertainment in my life. No more weekly parties, drinks, shopping sprees, binge watching T.V. shows, playing video games, hanging out, and wasting time. I chose freedom. I started reading two books a week, worked every day on my business, worked out daily, wrote every day, and made plans. It was all worth it.

Within two years, I was freer than I ever was. This type of purposeful living changed everything. I was no longer bored. I always had something useful to do. And that's how I still live my life.

My goal is to be free. And I realize that I can't be free if I waste my time on things that do not bring me closer to my goal. I want to make a contribution to society. I realize I can't do that if I'm weak. That's why I keep improving—mentally and physically. Nothing gives me more satisfaction than progress. When you give in to your desire to be free, you wake up ready to go every day. You can't wait to work on your freedom. Even in the beginning, when I moved back in with my parents, didn't have a car, and had little money, I knew I would be free. I was on the right path. That's the most important thing. You might not be free right now, but if you commit to freedom and stay on the path, you know you will get there. Only you know. It's a feeling that comes from your gut. You know that if you keep doing what you do, you will be free.

"Perhaps the biggest tragedy of our lives is that freedom is possible, yet we can pass our years trapped in the same old patterns."

—*Tara Brach*

CHAPTER NINETEEN

ANGER AND RESENTMENT

Some people walk around angry and resentful for days, weeks, and sometimes even years. That's because anger and resentment have a lot of power. They can easily consume you.

Today, I got involved in a fender bender at the car wash. Some guy hit the back of my car with his. My first response was anger. But like most civilized people, I contained myself and made arrangements with the guy that caused it. We exchanged contact information and I will send him the bill for the repairs. It's not a big deal and my car was only scratched a bit. But I noticed that I stayed angry after I drove off. "What a moron. He should learn how to drive. Idiot." I have to be honest, even though it happened this afternoon, I'm still a bit angry. I have to let it out somehow. I can't let it hold me captive. That's why

I'm telling you this story—I need to get it out of my system. Anger is a powerful emotion that can create a lot of darkness. That's why I never want to hold on to it.

Being angry is a habit. If you have the habit of getting angry, holding grudges, and becoming resentful, understand that you're not free. You're a prisoner of your emotions. In general, you don't want to be that way. And when it comes to anger, you really need to watch it. Becoming angry is normal. It happens to me too. **People who say they are never angry are either in denial or are total sociopaths. However, *staying* angry is not normal.** And often, we have a life that constantly makes us angry.

In that case, we don't need to change ourselves, we need to change our life. This is a delicate concept. I certainly don't believe you should complain and easily blame others for your anger. However, if you have a life that makes you angry, change your life. You can't get used to everything. I get that a lot of people are about accepting whatever happens to you. I'm also about accepting things you can't change. But if you live in a free country, you can *definitely* change your life. A big part of why I'm doing what I'm doing is because of anger.

When I lived in London I enjoyed it a lot, but at the same time, many things made me angry. Commuting on busy trains, the air pollution, the house prices, the shallow people I worked with. You know what I did? I didn't complain or judge. I removed myself from that place because I didn't have the resources at that time to solve my issues. For example, high house prices themselves are not a problem. But if you don't have the ability to buy the house you desire; it is a problem for *you*.

Remember, freedom has a price. If something angers you perpetually, you must do something about it. If you don't, the anger will build up inside of you, and you'll become a resentful person. You can fight and stand up for yourself without letting your soul turn dark. There are lines in life that one should not cross. You make up the lines. You can say, "Until here, and no further." When my ex-girlfriend could not be honest about small things in our relationship I gave it some time, but at a certain point I drew an imaginary line: No more lies. It sounds like a threat, and I have no problem if you interpret it that way. But that's who I am. I have a few important values that I never throw out of the window. No matter what. Why? Because your character is all you have.

If you look at successful nations and people you will find that those who value honesty are thriving. That's not a coincidence. When people have character and stand for what they believe in, you know their worth. Do you know why jerks bully others at work? It's because the other person doesn't fight back. We should all draw a line. Once it's crossed, we move on.

I never want to stay angry or negative. I want to enjoy my life. There is so much beauty here. And I enjoy small things. But when you're angry, you forget about everything. To be free, you need to give up anger. Commit to never staying angry for longer than is necessary. Let anger serve a purpose. Sometimes it's helpful. But mostly, it merely destroys your lust for life. Say goodbye to it. You're only screwing up your own life by being angry.

I already forgot about the fender bender. I'm not going to remain angry. Why? Because I'm committed to *living*.

"For every minute you remain angry, you give up sixty seconds of peace of mind."

— Ralph Waldo Emerson

CHAPTER TWENTY

EXPECTATIONS

To be truly a free spirit, you should have zero expectations. Most of us have expectations about everything. But we're often not aware that we do. We have expectations for our career, friends, partner, family, kids, and even how the world should work. Who are we to expect people to do what we want? Ever thought about that? If you take some time to think about expectations, you can't help but say they are delusional.

Secretly, we all expect all kinds of things. I expected my friends to help me with moving. I expected honesty from my co-workers. I expected my girlfriend to go running with me. I expected my mother to let go of me. I expected that readers of my blog all bought my book. I expected that I could find a beautiful apartment to buy. I expected to stay fit and not get injured.

But who am I to expect all those things? Sure, I can set goals. But I don't control outcomes. I only control my own effort. So why do I have expectations? It's another way of entering captivity. When you expect something from others and they don't live up to your expectations, you get disappointed, angry, or you judge them. None of this is helpful.

Being free means that you want freedom for others too. A free person is altruistic. A free person wishes the best for others. A free person wishes that others are free. And expectations are the enemy of freedom.

"But what if my family expects me to..." Become a doctor, have kids, or date so and so? So what? This is your life. If others can't accept that it will make you miserable to do something you despise, they don't know better. No need to get angry with others or try to lecture them. You can't convince people to adopt your beliefs (we'll get to that later). Just listen to them. But always do your own thing.

Even though you should always do what *you* decide, remember to listen before you make your decision. Only idiots don't listen. If you're 21 and want to quit college, at least listen to what your parents or people who were in your shoes have to say. If you're in a relationship and your best friend noticed some warning signs, hear her out.

A free person doesn't get offended by other people's views. If you want to be free, you should always be able to listen to people from all walks of life. Only unfree and angry people can't stand ideas that are different from theirs. But in the end, this is your life. You decide what you will do.

You listen to people, acknowledge them, especially if they are important to you, and finally: You make your decision. You and only you decide what's best for you. Often, people don't have all the information to give you advice. Your parents might expect you to become an engineer, but they might not know about your creative side. So when you set out to become an artist, make sure you become successful. Take it seriously and make a living. Get your shit together. And they will understand. If they don't, that's not your concern. Adults should mind their own business. And you should too.

"Freedom is independence of the compulsory will of another."

—Immanuel Kant

CHAPTER TWENTY-ONE

DEBT

I have a simple rule for myself: Always live below your means. I never borrowed money to buy something that wasn't necessary. The only thing that's necessary in life is food and shelter. You do whatever it takes to provide for those things. But you should never go into debt because you want a shiny car, buy fancy clothes, or go on a luxurious vacation. If you can't afford something, you don't buy it. It's very simple. And yet, we're all massively in debt.

This is one of the first rules I applied to my life. My parents were always in debt. And growing up, that took a toll on the family. The conversation was always about money. That created a strong aversion to debt for me. I can't tell you how much I hate debt. I'm willing to do anything to avoid it. Anything.

That's how committed I am to living debt free. I only have two exceptions: Student loans and mortgages. But again, I don't think you should take on more than you can. I bought my first apartment after I'd saved 40% of the property value in cash. But I didn't put everything down. In The Netherlands, you can buy property without putting money down. You only have to cover notary costs, property tax, and some other minor costs, which in total is about 5% of the property value. So if you buy a $200,000 home, you need at least $10,000 in cash. But if that's all you have, it's irresponsible to buy a home like that. You need a comfortable buffer of savings to be free of worry. A home requires maintenance and you need to pay property taxes. Also, banks in almost all countries work with a "loan to income value" of four. So if you make $50K, you can borrow $200K. All these ratios and calculations are here for a reason: To make debt responsible. You can borrow money rationally and buy a house you can afford. You can't say you are doing so rationally if you will be drowning in mortgage payments.

"But I can't afford a home in my city."

When I lived in London I also couldn't afford a home. I rented a small apartment and I couldn't buy. In many places, it's even better to rent. When rent prices are below the costs of buying, you should rent. No one says you *have* to buy. You should only buy if it's in your best interests and not just to say, "I bought a house." No one cares. Also, I'm not attached to any place. I'm attached to my freedom. If it's better for my freedom to move to another city or country, I will. And that's what I did. I moved back to my hometown so I could work on my writing career.

Do Whatever It Takes

I can't stress this enough. Never live from paycheck to paycheck longer than necessary. Life is not always a downhill road. I'm not saying you will never be in debt. I also accumulated student debt. And there will be months or years that you need to tighten your belt. But you should never accept that for your life. Always have a plan to get out of debt. Do not accept debt as a way of life.

When I got out of college, I was committed to paying off my student debt. The problem was that I made very little money. I started a business and I only made enough for my expenses. I even moved back in with my parents after I graduated. I couldn't afford a place. Actually, I didn't *want* to afford a place. I had a plan. I worked on my business all the time to get it off the ground because I knew that was the best long-term decision. I struggled for five years. FIVE. No savings, no property, no car. But gradually, I added some things to my life. I rented an apartment, bought a car, and started making a bit more money. I saved it. And before I bought anything of value in my life, I paid off all my student debt two years ago. Yes, it took me a long time. But I always knew it was coming (we'll talk about planning more in Part III).

Avoiding debt is about making decisions. You can decide not to buy an expensive car. You can decide to not buy a home. You can decide to commit to acquiring skills, improving yourself, starting a business, or getting a new job. You can achieve a lot over time. But it requires making tough choices. You can also decide to move to a different city or live close to your work.

You simply have to do whatever it takes to be free. And if that requires you to work hard for a few years, so what? Work extra shifts, get another job, start a business, whatever. Only watch for burn out. Even when I didn't make money with my business, I enjoyed my life. I enjoyed the struggle. That's the only secret to avoiding burn out. You must do something you choose and which you enjoy. That's the key. You *choose* to live below your means. If you do what you choose, you take pride in it. No one forces you to do anything. So don't do stupid things with your life. Always have a clear vision of freedom in your mind. Know why you're doing this. And you're already free.

"What can be added to the happiness of a man who is in health, out of debt, and has a clear conscience?"

— *Adam Smith*

CHAPTER TWENTY-TWO

UNWANTED HELP

I like to help people. It makes you feel useful. And I like to make myself useful. A lot of people want my help. But there are also a lot of people who don't. Or, the same people who want my help don't want it all the time. Many people who try to offer their help don't get that.

Sometimes you try to help, but people don't want it. That's not on them. That's on you. Why? Because you're offering help that's not wanted. You need to let people be. You must be free of your desire to help. Often, it's not even help. When we believe in something or think we know something, we want to share that with people. But maybe they are not waiting for you to come save them. Ever thought about that? Everyone has their own way of living. And we need to respect that.

I've learned to accept people for what they are. If they ask for help, I'm often ready to offer it. But it's all good regardless of anything. I don't expect anything from the people in my life. I also don't expect them to do what I do. I also don't expect that of you. You can do whatever you want with this book.

Convincing People Doesn't Work

A lot of our frustration with people comes from trying to convince others to do something. You see it a lot with parents and managers. "But he's not listening to me!"

Well, no one has *ever* listened to you. And no one listens to me either. That's simply the truth. Five hundred thousand people read my articles every month. No one listens to me though. Why? Because everyone makes their own decisions. Sure, I can inspire others with my actions and decisions. But ultimately, it's up to you to do something with it or not. But I'm good either way.

You have to be free of those types of expectations. Otherwise, you can never do good. You will always judge people. You will say people don't listen to you. But why would people listen anyway? Just because you're a parent or manager?

People care about themselves. And that's a good thing. You also care about yourself. So you can't expect people to do what you do.

You can only be concerned with doing the right thing. Set the right example, do what you have to, live well, and always do your best. If others want to screw up, gossip, be lazy, complain, and manipulate, let them. You can't help people who don't want help. It's the hard truth. And if you're not willing to accept that, you can never be truly free of social restrictions.

Once I gave up offering unwanted help and trying to convince people, I became free. I'm only concerned with doing the right thing. If your kids don't listen to you, you can't blame them or treat them differently. Neither can you blame your parents if they never change.

People are what they are. That doesn't mean people don't change. It means only *they* can decide to make a change. It's the same for you. Why do you do what you do? It's because you decided it, right? You need to give yourself credit for that. It's not because of other people.

No matter how inspiring someone is, you're the one who has to *do* everything. That's what I always say to readers who thank me for changing their lives. There's no such thing. I can't change another person's life. Only *you* can change your life.

We often focus on what *we* do for others. "I do all this for him!" We think people owe us something if we do something for them. Why should others owe us anything? And why would you owe others something?

Only be concerned with doing the right thing. You can't do anything else. Accept that reality and you will never be concerned with what others do with your help.

"Men talk of freedom! How many are free to think? Free from fear, from perturbation, from prejudice? Nine hundred and ninety-nine in a thousand are perfect slaves."

— *Henry David Thoreau*

CHAPTER TWENTY-THREE

DEFENDING MY IDEAS

I used to have the urge to defend myself every time my ideas were attacked. People disagree with you all the time at work, at home, at the gym. When you're concerned with defending yourself, you're not accepting different points of view. You're not allowing others to be free. And a big part of freedom is to accept that others are also free. Remember, freedom is to do what you want and be as you are. You can't do that if you're constantly defending yourself. **True freedom means you're not concerned with other people's opinions, views, and actions. You also don't have the need to explain why your ideas and actions are the best.**

There's no such thing as "best" so and so. What works for you might not work for someone else. You need to be free of your ego. You don't need to prove people wrong. You also don't need to show people how smart you are. The wiser you are, the less you feel like showing it to others. A free and wise person does what they think is right. And they will question everything. So there's no need to explain yourself to others who don't understand you.

Since I gave up defending my ideas, I'm free to think and do whatever I want. I know that I'm driven by my core values and morality. I don't do things that harm the common good. As long as I abide by those rules, I have no need to explain my ideas.

Every week, rude and aggressive people email me about my articles. They disagree with the things I write and are not looking for a discussion. They simply want to defend their point of view. I used to respond to a lot of those emails. But I simply don't have the need to engage in a battle with those folks.

We're only trying to defend our ideas. Also, I can't convince them. If I *could*, I would've done it with the article. I say what I have to say, and beyond that, there's not much to say. So what if someone disagrees? They have every right. But when people are idiots, sometimes I tell them.

One guy recently said that I should stop quoting Marcus Aurelius because he was an emperor that killed people. I told him to grow up. It doesn't require a genius to understand that historical figures did a lot of wrong things. Today, we live in a transparent society and you can't do that stuff. Ancient philosophers said and did a lot of dumb shit. Does that mean we should discard their good ideas? Of course not. We can learn from everything.

That's how I look at it. If others don't agree; so what? It doesn't mean you're wrong. It also doesn't mean the other person is right. If you stay humble and keep challenging your ideas, you will keep learning. That's what matters.

Don't Become Attached To Ideas

A lot of people defend their beliefs because they *become* their beliefs. When someone attacks their ideas, they feel *they* are attacked. They *need* to defend themselves. That's the opposite of being free. When you're free, you're not attached to any idea.

I'm not attached to any one of my ideas. If I come across something that works better, I abandon my old ideas. I'm loyal to family and close friends, but not to ideas. Ideas are cheap. Everyone can come up with them.

I'm concerned with what *works* in practice. If you have a better way of living or doing something, I will listen. But ultimately, I make the decision to act on it or not.

You need to do your own thing. Everyone is different. The problem is that everyone tries to convince us that their beliefs are the best. They want to make you something you're not.

Never give in. Always be yourself. That's the only honorable way of going through your life—as yourself.

"To be yourself in a world that is constantly trying to make you something else is the greatest accomplishment."

— Ralph Waldo Emerson

CHAPTER TWENTY-FOUR

FORCED HAPPINESS

A few years ago, I gave up my excessive drive to always be happy. I used to think that the purpose of life was happiness. But that philosophy didn't work for me. I realized that happiness is always a byproduct. When you spend time with people you love, you feel happy. When you invest four years in getting a degree, you feel happy and accomplished when you graduate. You feel happy when you come up with a useful idea at work. You feel happy when you finish a hard workout. You feel happy when you listen to good music. Happiness comes from within. It's the feeling you get from an action. It can be as simple as having a conversation with someone or listening to a song.

But happiness doesn't last. It's a feeling that comes and goes.

Some people disagree with that and say you can always be happy. I think you can be happy the *majority* of time. Why? Because you need to build a good life for yourself. A life that makes you happy. No one is truly happy when you live a shitty life of your own doing. I genuinely believe that. If you live below your potential, give up on life, and don't reach for something better, you will be miserable.

In contrast, if you've built a life you're in control of and have goals you're working towards, you will be happy no matter what. Almost everything makes you happy. I have a simple life. On an average day, I'll work for 4-5 hours, workout for 60-90 minutes, read an hour, have dinner with my family, and have enough time to take care of necessary stuff like doing groceries, cleaning my house, doing laundry, etc. You wouldn't believe how much time you have to take care of everything if you work 1-2 hours less than average people.

By contrast, I work 7 days a week. So I put in the same amount of time as people who work 9-5. Also, I'm more effective. When I work 4-5 hours, I *work*. I don't mess around or browse social media. My habits used to be different when I worked in a crowded office. But I've created both a life and career that give me more freedom. "But you don't have kids," is what some people say. If I get kids, I have the freedom to change my schedule. Free people do what they want. The people who use their kids as an excuse can also be free. In fact, I personally know several free people with kids. One of my friends even has 3 kids. He also has a job, but his boss gives him a lot of freedom. He made arrangements with him.

A lot of people assume you have to work for yourself to be free. That's not true. If you're employed, your company or organization wants you to do your job. If you're happy and free, you do a better job. That's why it's important to have an open discussion at your workplace about the way you work and live. My friend drops off his kids at school and comes home for lunch. He has enough freedom to enjoy his life. That wasn't always the case. Just two years ago he complained a lot. But now his life has more balance because he made a few clear decisions. He didn't even switch jobs. He simply committed to freedom. That means no more spending time with negative co-workers. Instead, he's doing his best and prioritizing family and health. He no longer hangs out with everybody he knows. He works, spends time with his family, and goes to the gym. That's his decision. Sure, he can't pick up his kids from school when they are done, but he has peace with that. He's still around a lot in the morning and for lunch. You can't have everything. But as long as you have freedom, you will be happy.

Shitty Times

If you're unhappy or frustrated it doesn't mean you should become impatient and quit everything. Remember, always seek the truth and don't be afraid to do hard things. If you're unhappy, a different job or city is not the answer. We all know that. You can travel to every country in the world, but if you don't have inner peace, your problems will follow you wherever you go. Life is the same for every individual. We all have to wake up, eat, wash, go to the toilet. We will all experience death, loss, and grief. We all get rejected. We all get injured and ill. And money will not change anything about being human. Sometimes we forget that. See this as a reminder that you will always be human regardless of your circumstances. Regardless of how bad life is at times, these moments always pass. Time moves in one direction. And even the worst times are not here to stay. If you're unhappy, you don't have to fight it. Accept it. And go through it. Know that everything will pass. That's also true for good times. Everything we do or experience is temporarily. Nothing good or bad about that. It's merely how life works. Once we accept that, we become free from trying to change how our life is *during a specific moment.* Some things we have to endure. But it doesn't mean that you can't change your life. Since all life situations are temporary, you get a new chance every hour and day. You can commit to making your life better. You can commit to being free. Then, you have to execute it.

"When you are content to be simply yourself and don't compare or compete, everyone will respect you."

— Lao Tzu

THE FREEDOM PLAN

"Freedom is what you do with what's been done to you."

—Jean-Paul Sartre

CHAPTER TWENTY-FIVE

PLANNING IS EVERYTHING

Wishing, hoping, wanting, talking—it's all useless without action. And to become free, you need *a lot* of action. While taking action is better than doing nothing or dreaming, **action without thought is a waste of effort.** For years, I had a strong urge to be free, and I took a lot of action. I said yes to every opportunity, traveled a lot, did a lot of different types of work. But I wasn't precise in my actions. I didn't have a thought-out plan.

Planning is not only important if you want to achieve results. Planning for failure is what keeps you going. While most people give up when they experience setbacks, a person with a plan knows what to do.

That's true freedom—to always know what to do, no matter

what the situation is. Everything you've read until now will fade if you don't put it in practice. I'm sure you know this. **How many books have you read? And how many of the ideas that you learned are you still applying today?** My goal for this book is to not be like other books you read once and forget. I hope you *live* the ideas we talk about. That requires execution and planning. Otherwise, we can never be free.

I read two books a week. That's over 100 a year. And most books give you good ideas and inspiration. But that always fades. So instead of saying goodbye to you right here and letting you create your own plan, I'm sharing an action plan with you.

We've talked a lot about why freedom matters. And why we need to give up a lot of things so we can be free. But *how* do you execute those things? *How* can you be free? That's what Part III is about. My goal is to connect with as many of you as I can. If you'd like to connect to me, and other readers, I invite you to do the following:

Post this quote on any social media you currently use:

"Through discipline comes freedom." —*Aristotle*

And in the description, add #whatitakestobefree so other readers and I can find your post. You can also tag me in the post. It's not about showing off or trying to impress others. I'm not a big social media user myself. I only like to use it to connect with others.

Most importantly, this is about accountability and connecting with other like-minded people. Books are static and it's impossible to interact with each other. You can't interact with me or other readers through this book. For some people that's okay, because they prefer to process ideas alone. But others have a desire to find counterparts who share the same values. That's especially important if the people around you are not thinking and working on the same things as you. By searching on that hashtag, others can find you. And you can find others that are on the same path. We can use this challenge to connect and support one another.

Remember, you can do whatever you want. You can keep everything to yourself. Or, if you want to post on social media, you can post another quote or something different. Either way, I will search for #whatitakestobefree on social media to encourage everyone who posted about it.

How To Read Part III

Part III consists of exercises I did and actions I took to become free. I'm sharing what *I* did to become free. You don't have to do the same. My goal is to demonstrate my way of thinking. Freedom has a price and we have to take a lot of action to become free. The last thing I want is to only motivate or inspire you. Because that stuff never lasts.

Too often, plans, challenges, and exercises you read about in books are not executed. Of course, whether you apply this stuff or not is up to you. The exercises and actions in Part III are based on what I've personally done to find freedom. In other words, Part III is my actual plan for freedom. I'm still executing some parts of it. It's not something I made up to make this book look better. No, it's stuff I actually do. Let's start.

"Success depends upon previous preparation, and without such preparation there is sure to be failure."

— Confucius

CHAPTER TWENTY-SIX

ESTABLISH YOUR CORE VALUES

Freedom comes from knowing who you are. Only then can you do what you like. So the first step to becoming free is getting clear on who you are. It's the foundation of a free life. If you don't know who you are, you can't seek out people who are like you. You also won't be able to find a compatible partner. Or, if you have a partner, you won't be able to be free inside the relationship. You can't expect others to smell who you are. You need to tell others about your values. It's not fair to tell people, "You don't understand me!" if you don't give them a chance.

EXERCISE: Sit down with a pen and paper and write down

what you value in life.

While the exercise is straightforward, the process of establishing your values never ends. I continuously examine my values. I want to get down to the bottom of who I am even though I don't believe you can ever expect to know yourself 100%. Even if it's possible, I like to think it's not. I never want to definitively say, "This is who am I forever." You can decide to change at any point if you decide doing so will make your life better.

See this exercise as a *start*. No one expects you to be able to identify and articulate your ultimate set of core values here. Come up with things you value right now. Look at it this way: Your goal is to be free. What values will help you achieve that? Here are my values:

1. **Authenticity**—Be the same person at every occasion in life. Don't act differently in front of your parents, friends, co-workers, in-laws, and strangers. Stay your true self. And never be afraid of other people's judgments.

2. **Truthfulness**—Tell the truth. Always. Especially when it comes to your own life. Don't have money? Don't pretend you're wealthy. Never went to college? Own it. Be honest about who you are and what you've done. You'll be able to look at yourself in the mirror with pride.

3. **Joyfulness**—Life is short. Do things that bring you joy. And NEVER do something you hate for longer than is necessary. Enjoy the small things. Music, other people, working out, walking, laying down, reading, and so forth.

4. **Curiosity**—Get to the bottom of everything you do. Not because you must. But because it's fun to know things. Life is fascinating. Acknowledge it. And then, try to understand it. But leave it at trying. Even though some things can't be understood, you can still admire them.

5. **Responsibility**—Own your actions, mistakes, and current life situation. Understand what's in your control, and fully own it. Don't like something? Change it. But don't take responsibility for things that are not on your plate. Focus on yourself. What other adults do is not your concern, nor your responsibility.

6. **Love**—Build intimate and deep relationships with a few people. Depth matters more than breadth. Spend more time with your spouse than your co-workers. Get to know your siblings on a deeper level. Choose two or three friends to spend your time with. Love your family. The people you see every day should get your highest priority.

7. **Fearlessness**—Don't fear the future. And don't be afraid of what people you don't care about think of you. Only care about what you and the people you love

think about you. Everything else is noise. Have dignity. Do the right thing and don't fear the rest.

8. **Loyalty**—Even though you might not see your old friends, co-workers, team members, stay loyal. Once you build a bond with someone, don't break it unless it's necessary. But most importantly, stay loyal to yourself. Never sacrifice your own mental well-being for others. Treat yourself like you treat someone you love.

As you can see, **I don't consider personal freedom a value. It's my goal. And my values help me to get there.** For example, my sense of responsibility helps me save my money and treat people with respect. My fearlessness helps me take bold action and stand up for myself. I'm not afraid to slap a bully's face. I value kindness, but I fight fire with fire. That's simply who I am. I'm comfortable with that and I will accept the consequences.

I have uncovered my values over the past four years. And the list above hasn't changed much since I crafted it. Looking back, I've always demonstrated the values. However, I didn't live by them clearly. For example, I value truthfulness. But my ex-girlfriend was raised in a different way. In her culture and family, telling the truth wasn't important. It was normal to tell white lies. When a family member passed away, they wouldn't tell some people for months because they were afraid of hurting their feelings. That's the opposite of the way I was raised and how I looked at the world. If I had been "living by my values" at the time, I would never have started the relationship since I knew her values didn't align with mine.

If you value authenticity, you'll have a difficult time in the entertainment business. It's filled with fake people. You will be miserable. So this exercise is not only about establishing your core values. It's also about sticking to them.

Actions:

1. Open a Word document or note on your favorite note-taking app
2. List a maximum of 10 core values
3. Explain what you mean for each value in two or three sentences
4. Print your list and put it on your desk or digitally pin it at the top of your favorites in your app
5. Read your values every day for the next 14 days

"The man who has no inner life is a slave to his surroundings."

— *Henri-Frederic Amiel*

CHAPTER TWENTY-SEVEN

THE "I CAN ALWAYS..." TECHNIQUE

This exercise helps you to get comfortable with uncertainty. I call this the "I can always..." technique. I used it when I quit my job in 2015 and took a step back from my family business. I wanted to earn a living as a writer and be free to do what I want.

Like everyone who starts something new, I started from 0. I had nothing. No website, no social media, no followers, no readers. There was a lot of uncertainty and that caused a lot of worry. The good thing about starting from nothing is that you have a clean slate. I could try a lot of things. But at the same time, I also had thoughts like, "What if this fails? What if I go broke?" To battle my insecurity and anxiety, I came up with this technique. It goes like this:

1. Open your notebook or note taking app

2. Think about the work you've done in the past

3. What skills have you acquired? Think carefully about the type of work you've done and what you learned. Too often, we just look at job titles. "I was just a store attendant." No, you learned sales and communication skills.

4. Write down the skills you acquired

5. Now, think about all the potential jobs that you *could* do

6. Simply, write "I can always..."

7. Then list everything you can think of

Here's what I came up with: "I can always work in sales at any company, build websites for people or organizations, work at any store, become a teacher, work as a copywriter, work remotely for companies all over the world, buy and sell popular products, etc."

There's a lot you can do to make money so you can pay the bills. There's no need to worry about that stuff if you're willing to do any job. **You can't control most things in life, but you can control your will to succeed. If you're willing to do whatever it takes, you will.**

Taking some time to think about all the things you could potentially do to survive will help you relax. The goal, though, is not just to survive. You want to be free, which obviously requires work. Simultaneously, you don't need to fear failure. There's always something you can do.

"For a man to act himself, he must be perfectly free; otherwise he is in danger of losing all sense of responsibility or of self-respect."

— Henry David Thoreau

CHAPTER TWENTY-EIGHT

SET GOALS FOR EVERY AREA OF YOUR LIFE

If you're committed to freedom, you're pursuing the highest achievable goal in life. It's funny to me how people pretend that being free is easy. They say they just want a simple life. "I don't need much." Well, that's the highest aim in life! There's nothing easy about achieving freedom. You know what's easy? Complaining, being ungrateful, consumerism, being angry, and doing nothing—all those things are easier than striving for freedom. So if you're committed to achieving freedom, know that you're after something hard. And that's a great thing. Why would you aim low?

Since freedom is such a high aim, I like to set smaller goals that help me achieve my overall goal, to be free. That's how I look at goals. My main goal is to be free. And all my other goals contribute to living the way I want. I realize that it's a high aim and that freedom doesn't come easy. That's why I'm big on setting small goals. In the past, I would set goals I didn't control. "I want to make a million bucks," was one of those goals.

The thing is; **I don't control the rewards I get. What do I control? My effort.** That's why now I set goals for things I control. For example, here are some of my goals:

- Publish at least one article a week

- Launch two new courses this year

- Read two books a week

- Save at least 30% of my money

- Work out every day

- Spend at least 30 minutes a day improving my writing skills

If I fail to achieve those goals it's because I didn't execute. In contrast, if I would set a goal like, "Make X dollars with your next course launch" I would be focusing on something I don't entirely control. Sure, I control the quality of my course and how well I market it, but I don't control the people who buy it; you can't force someone to buy your product.

Well, you can, but you'd be committing a crime. I have values and never act irresponsibly. I stay ethical. And I focus on what

I control.

I'm a big fan of setting small goals because it gives you direction. If you're often aimless, setting goals can be especially beneficial. **I like setting goals for every area of my life. To me, these areas are career, health, learning, money, and relationships.**

However, you don't *need* to set goals. If you work well without them, that's great. Health and learning goals are the most important areas of life to me. A big part of becoming free is to acquire skills that you can always rely on. That requires a learning strategy. First, you need to establish *what* skills you will acquire or improve. Second, you need to establish *how* you will go about acquiring and improving your skills.

Remember to acquire skills you're passionate about. And focus on things you have a natural talent for. Life is better when you do things you're good at *and* enjoy doing. That's the only way you get pleasure out of doing work. Plus, when you do something you're good at, you can provide more value. That will not only benefit yourself; it will also help others.

But we can't be of value if we don't improve ourselves. **Continuous improvement is the only way to stay relevant. That's why learning equals freedom.**

Freedom to do any type of work you want. Why? Simply because you're good at it. In contrast, if you're not good at anything, you're also not free. You will be forced to do work you don't enjoy. Investing in yourself helps you to avoid that. It will set you free.

A Pen And Paper

That's all you need. You can put away this book right now and set goals for yourself. Sit down for 10 minutes, and think about this:

- What are your goals for this week?

- What are your goals for this month?

- What are your goals for this year?

- What are your goals for next year?

- What are your 3-year goals?

- What are your 5-year goals?

You don't have to answer all these questions. Plus, your 3- and 5-year goals will probably change along the way. The purpose of these long-term goals is to give you perspective. When you move into a direction, it's easy to make adjustments. I've often adapted my long-term goals. But I'm glad I set those goals because if I didn't, I probably wouldn't be where I am today. The thing is, when you're motionless, you're more likely to *stay* motionless.

That's the purpose of setting goals—to get you moving towards something. Some people don't like to look ahead more than a month. That's fine. Do whatever works for you. When do you know if something works? When you do something that gives you a *clear* sense of direction. If you get that feeling, you're on to something.

"Our goals can only be reached through a vehicle of a plan, in which we must fervently believe, and upon which we must vigorously act. There is no other route to success."

— *Pablo Picasso*

CHAPTER TWENTY-NINE

BUILD YOUR FREEDOM FUND

Freedom in the modern world is related to money, a lot. Even though we all want to minimize the role that money plays in our life, we can't run away from paying our bills. I don't have to tell you that the best things in life are free. However, food and shelter are *not* free. We need money but shouldn't fear it. Because often, money related issues cause stress. That's why we need to do everything possible to avoid living from paycheck to paycheck. Instead, you want to have what I call a Freedom Fund. It's a pile of cash you can always fall back on for either small or big things. From replacing your dishwasher to saying no to your boss. To live as you are, you need a strong foundation. You need to know who you are and what your core values are. Plus, you need to have some cash so you can sleep comfortably at night. That's what your Freedom Fund is for. If you're starting from 0, do this:

Phase 1: From Nothing To Something

Do whatever it takes to save at least one month of expenses. Live lean, take on extra shifts, work more, sell stuff you don't need, etc. You don't have to track your expenses to the penny. Simply take the time once to calculate how much you spend every month on necessities. When I talk about necessities, I'm talking about rent or mortgage, insurances, utilities, food, and transportation. Depending on where you live, you might get scared at how much it costs to simply live. But don't worry about the number. Phase 1 is all about awareness. Too many of us are not aware of how much *need* to spend.

Phase 2: Not Spending Money On BS

Don't think about buying clothes or going to restaurants while you're saving for phase 1. If you have debt, you also don't need to think about paying off the whole amount. Just pay off the minimum monthly amount. Phase 2 is all about managing your spending behavior. Regularly ask yourself, "Do I really want to trade my hard-earned cash for this?" Often, the answer is, "No, choose freedom."

Phase 3: Getting Comfortable

Once you've saved up at least one month of expenses, aim for saving six months of expenses. During this time you can relax more and spend some money on yourself. But never save less than 30% during this phase. It's important to quickly get to a nice cushion.

Phase 4: Growth

So you've saved at least six months of expenses. Now, put it away in a savings account and don't touch it. Everything you save from now on is meant for investing. Remember that you don't need to think about investing your money until you've got that six months of expenses. I still recommend saving 30%.

Phase 5: Freedom

In this phase you have enough cash and investments to cover your cost of living. In the beginning, you can make huge leaps if you go from nothing to something. Most people accept the status quo when they are comfortable. It's not a bad position. You have enough cash to buy small things or go on vacations. But you still need to work. At phase 5, you don't *need* to do anything.

We all want to get there. But if you're in Phase 1-3, your focus is to build your Freedom Fund. It's simply a savings account that you wire cash to every single month. If you don't have it yet, set it up today. Then, deposit any excess cash you have. Doesn't matter whether it's $5 or $500. This way of looking at financial freedom works well for me. I'm not the type that tracks every penny or wants to stress about personal finance. Too often, people are obsessed with personal finance. They read about it every day, look at their spending multiple times a day, and freak out when they have to spend their cash on something big. I don't want that. I want to be free even if I'm not 100% financially free. See, personal finance is like philosophy. Everybody has a different way of looking at life, but also at money. This book is not about investing, paying off your debt, or managing your money. This book is about personal freedom and getting comfortable with uncertainty. The truth is that personal finance is easy once you take some time to learn about it. Basically, everything is common sense. You know everything I've mentioned in this chapter. The challenge is executing it. When you see a nice watch, shirt, or any other shiny object you like, it's difficult to resist buying it. Most of us can buy that stuff if we want. You either use your savings account, credit card, or get a loan. It's very simple. It's way harder to *not* buy. **Businesses only have one objective: To sell you stuff. But remember that you're the one who's in control.** You manage your wallet. Do you want to trade your money for captivity? Of course not. You want freedom.

"Few people have any next, they live from hand to mouth without a plan, and are always at the end of their line."

— *Ralph Waldo Emerson*

CHAPTER THIRTY

ELIMINATE WHAT MAKES YOU MISERABLE

Too often, we live without thinking about what we do and how we spend our time. That's how we *create* an unfree life for ourselves. Remember, we are the ruler of our own kingdom. **If we have a life that makes us unhappy, *we're* responsible for it. It's because we made certain decisions.**

We all have habits and beliefs that don't serve us. We accumulate many things through life. But to be free, we need to be light on our feet. We can't have a burden. We need to get rid of things that make us miserable. This exercise forces you to reexamine everything you do. Sit down with a pen and notebook or your note-taking app. You can also use the whitespace in this book to write. List all the things in your life that make you miserable:

Work: What do you dislike about your work?

....

Habits: What do you repeatedly do that has a negative impact on your life?

....

Beliefs: What thought patterns limit you in life?

....

Possessions: What are some possessions that are a burden?

....

People you spend time with: Who drains your energy?

....

What you eat: What does your diet look like? What food makes you feel bad?

....

Sleep: With how many hours of sleep do you feel tired? What time do you go to bed? What time do you wake up?

....

Now, do one of the following:

1. **Change**—For example, if you don't like your job, you don't necessarily have to quit. If you still like your co-workers or the industry, you can try to change your role or your attitude.

2. **Eliminate**—Everything that makes you miserable that *can* be eliminated, *needs* to be eliminated. Bad habits, useless possessions, expensive cars, unnecessary subscriptions, you name it. Get rid of it. Elimination doesn't count for people. That's the premise of the book and movie, American Psycho. That's not what we do. However, you *can* stop spending time with people who drain your energy. You might not want to cut toxic family members out of your life. In that case, minimize the impact they have on you. Avoid them as much as possible.

The key is that you need to take action if your life is not the way you want. If you don't like your job, decide to get rid of it. You don't have to do it right now. This exercise helps you to *design* your life. Most people who quit their job already decided to do so six months or a year before they handed in their resignation. In the meantime, they disconnected mentally, thought about what they wanted to do next, improved their skills, and then found another job or started a business.

This exercise also helps you examine everything you do; which can be scary to some people. They feel uncomfortable saying goodbye to people, jobs, or possessions. Remember, you don't *have* to do anything. Just realize that this is your life and you're responsible for yourself. I would be more scared about living an unhappy and unfree life. You know, life is long. What hurts more? The temporary pain of loneliness and disappointing people, or being unfree for a lifetime?

"Liberty, taking the word in its concrete sense, consists in the ability to choose."

— *Simone Weil*

CHAPTER THIRTY-ONE

GET MOVING

Life is hard—mentally and physically. Taking action is not only a mental thing. Starting a business, moving to a different city or country, buying a house, raising kids, you need your body to *do* all those things. The stronger you are, the easier it will be for you to do all those things. Even though there's no need to convince you of all the benefits of exercise, I can say this: **Working out doesn't only make you stronger so you can deal better with the stresses and uncertainties of life—it will also give you more energy.** The challenge most people face is making *time* to exercise.

I challenge you to put daily exercise at the top of your list of priorities. It should be there together with sleep and food. Exercise should come before work. Yes, exercising is more important than making more money. If it requires you to work a bit less, then so what? Your health is more important. Wake up earlier, watch less T.V., hang out less—do whatever it takes to exercise more. Here's how I prioritize daily exercise:

Step 1: Decide what type of exercise you will do. Pick one or two activities. I either run or go to the gym. Keep it simple. No need to do different things. Pick something you enjoy that is easy to do.

Step 2: Create a weekly schedule. Aim for daily exercise. Schedule your workouts in advance on your calendar.

Step 3: Make it easy for you to work out. I prefer working out in the morning. I put my workout clothes in my bedroom, so I see them in the morning.

Step 4: Workout at 80% of your max. You don't need to win at the Olympics. You work out to get energy and to *not* get injured.

Step 5: When your body aches, take rest. Your goal is to *aim* for daily exercise. If you work out five times a week, you're exercising more than average people. It's important to listen to your body and build up the intensity. But in general, I never take long breaks unless I'm sick or injured.

The fitter you are, the more freedom you will have to do what you want. What if you're injured or chronically ill? Don't give up and accept a life of pain. Do what you *can*. You're not in a competition with anyone. You do this for yourself. A healthy person is a free person. We don't value it enough. We only miss it when we don't have it anymore. Once I decided to prioritize my health over almost everything in life, I felt free. I'd rather chase health than chase money. We all know that more money won't make you feel good once you're financially free. But you can never be healthy enough. You can always improve your diet, sleep, and exercise. So get moving.

"It is a shame for a man to grow old without seeing the beauty and strength of which his body is capable."

— Socrates

CHAPTER THIRTY-TWO

SYSTEMIZE YOUR FI-NANCES

Life is a lot simpler when you have a system that supports your financial goals. A system is nothing more than a combination of rules that contribute to a single goal. Often, the rules are automated. Let me give you an example of how I organize my bank accounts. I have three of them. Why not one? When you use one account for everything, it's difficult to get a grip on your finances. And when you don't have a grip, it's difficult to create rules. That's why I'm a proponent of three bank accounts. Here's how I use my accounts:

1. **The normal checking account**—My rule is to always keep less than $800 in this account. I only use this account

to cover groceries and other small purchases. This makes it difficult for me to make big purchases. Every time I want to buy something that's more than several hundred dollars, I need to transfer money from my savings account. Guess what happens? I think to myself, "It's not worth it." That's how I've saved myself from buying a lot of crap.

2. **The fixed costs account**—I created a separate bank account for my fixed costs and always make sure there's enough money in that account to cover my mortgage and bills for six months. You can calculate your fixed costs once and then set up automatic payments from your checking account. I don't use this account for anything else. This also gives you a clear view of how much your cost of living is. Most banks allow you to have multiple accounts at no additional cost. You don't even need an ATM card for your fixed costs account. You're not making physical payments with it. Once I created this account, I went to the websites of the companies through which I pay my mortgage and utility bills, and changed my bank account. I don't pay anything manually. You just have to set this thing up once and you're done.

3. **The savings account**—I wire a set amount from my checking account to my savings account every month. You can also set up automatic payments for this.

This three-account strategy helps you to get an instant view of your financial health. But you don't have to feel guilty about spending the money that's left in your checking account. If you stick to your rules, pay your fixed costs first, and wire cash to your savings account, you can spend what's left in your checking account. Poor people do the opposite. They spend their income first, and then try to pay the bills with what's left.

Another example of systemizing your finances is to set up automatic payments for your credit card(s) and loans. I'm not against credit cards. I'm against personal debt. I use a credit card, but I don't treat it like a credit line. I've set up automatic payments for my credit card so I don't pay interest. You can sign up for automatic payments online and agree to allow the card company to debit your payment from your bank account on a set date each month. If you don't have money, you can't spend it.

Always think in systems. Think to yourself: "How can I automate everything that's money related?" If you have other loans, set up automatic payments so you don't have to think about it anymore. Make the payments from your fixed costs account because until you pay off a loan, you *need* to make your payments.

It takes some time to make all these calculations and set up three accounts, but once you've done it, you'll be in control. These rules truly help me live below my means. It also helps me to never get into debt.

You see, it doesn't take much to systemize your finances. It might seem like a lot if you're reading this. But trust me, it takes one afternoon to take care of everything I talked about. Sometimes we just have to sit down with a computer and get it over with. I know that confronting yourself with your financial situation is painful and you want to put it off until tomorrow. But you and I both know that doesn't mean we can run away from our responsibilities. Once you get it done, you'll be more in control of your financial situation. And control is what makes you free.

"Unless commitment is made, there are only promises and hopes; but no plans."

— *Peter F. Drucker*

CHAPTER THIRTY-THREE

MEDITATE ON WHAT COULD GO WRONG

No matter how prepared you are and how much you plan, things will still go wrong. Often, people say, "I'll deal with a setback when it happens." It's a better mindset than always worrying about everything that could happen. However, it's also naïve. We all know that we will have setbacks and hurt sooner or later. But when all is well, we don't want to think about. Oddly enough, good times are *perfect* for preparation. When everything in your life is going well, you can take the time focus on what you want to do to improve yourself.

In contrast, when you're in the middle of a personal crisis, you *don't* have the time or energy to strengthen your mind and body. You need all your resources to make the best of what's in front of you. It's not a matter of *if* a setback will hit you, it's a matter of *when*. At some point, we all have to deal with death and grief. We all experience downs in our relationships. We all face personal crises and feeling down for no particular reason.

And these obstacles never come at a good time. When something bad happened to me I always said, "Why now?!" As if I had any control over external factors. It's such a delusional thing to say and think. What? Just because everything is going well for you, you are entitled to continued success? **We're entitled to nothing.** That's why this exercise is so important. When everything is going well, you want to meditate on what could go wrong. Let's do a thought exercise.

1. Find a comfortable place to sit or lie down

2. Close your eyes

3. Think about a person that's close to you and who you rely on for support

4. Imagine having a good time with them

5. Feel the joy you experience from being with that person

6. Now, imagine that you're alone in a room

7. Imagine you're receiving a call from someone

8. You pick up the phone

9. The person you love just died

10. Feel the sadness in your stomach

Now, snap out of it. It's not necessary to get stuck in that feeling. The point is to *temporarily* feel negative emotions, so you don't experience shock when you have to deal with grief in the future. Repeat this exercise for whatever you fear. I regularly meditate on losing my business and money. I imagine that I made a wrong investment and that everything is gone. I've done that so often in my mind that if it happens, it's not new to me. I will be ready to start over.

I also meditate on getting ill or injured. What will I do when I can't walk? All this stuff might sound depressing to you. Or you might think, "That would never happen to me." How are you so sure? Isn't it better to take five minutes to prepare? If it happens, you will be prepared. And if it doesn't happen, you didn't lose anything. You only gained mental strength.

"I am prepared for the worst, but hope for the best."

— *Benjamin Disraeli*

CHAPTER THIRTY-FOUR

INVEST WHEN YOU'RE READY

Unless you're pursuing a full-time career in investing, the purpose of investing is not to make money. Freedom is to do what you want. And if you don't like investing, you can still build wealth. Too often we assume we can instantly make passive income by investing our money. But where does that initial money come from? You can borrow money, but that always comes at a price.

When you borrow money, you're obligated to pay it back. Borrowing money to invest in the stock market or real estate is not free. No one will give you money for free. We all know that. And yet, we believe in investing in fairy tales. The free person needs to find a sure way to generate money. I believe that the best way to do that is by starting a business. I want to stress that it's not the *only* way. I prefer owning my own business because it gives me more control and freedom. It also comes with more risk and responsibility. The point is not *how* you make money. It's important to realize that we need to generate value to generate income.

Too often, we get ahead of ourselves by imagining a financially free life. But I believe in *earning* freedom. Once I improved my skills, started to generate money, was debt free, and created my Freedom Fund, I started investing. In that order. Investing is the last step towards freedom. So if you're still working on the first steps, I would forget about investing for now.

Just realize that investing is not a way to make money for most of us. It sounds counterintuitive, but your decision to ignore investing will save you a lot of time and money. Too often, we waste our time on pursuing financial "opportunities." When you don't have enough savings and are putting your money in specific stocks, timeshares, bitcoin, or gold, you're wasting your energy. Financial "experts" promise that you will make money with investing. In reality, it's not that easy.

The purpose of your career or business is to make money. You see? First, you make money, then, you invest it. That's how you build wealth. At least, this is the most responsible strategy. And it's the strategy I pursue. I didn't seriously think about investing until two years ago. Until then, I was too focused on building a sustainable career and saving my money.

But that doesn't mean you should completely ignore investing. I recommend learning more about investing as you are working and saving your money.

Here are the steps I took to get started with investing:

1. I started reading about the different ways people invest: Stocks, index funds, mutual funds, 401K, real estate, businesses, etc.

2. I read books and articles (see the further reading section at the end of this book for book recommendations).

3. I sought out real estate investors I personally knew to learn more about their strategies. I think that real estate investing is one of the few things you can't learn from books. You need to talk to people in your city and country. And you need to look at a lot of properties to understand what's important to profitable real estate investing.

4. Step one through three took me three to four years. It's a slow process but you need to start as early as you can.

5. Once I learned more about investing, I decided to only focus on local real estate (because I know my city) and index funds. I've eliminated everything else. No mutual funds, no single stocks, no bitcoin, no exotic investments, nothing overseas.

6. I've narrowed down my investment strategy even more. I only invest in the Vanguard S&P500 index fund. No bonds or other index funds for now.

7. When it comes to property, I'm currently focused on one-bedroom apartments in the city center because there's always been a high demand. My city has two universities and a lot of young folks who are looking for one-bedroom apartments.

Everybody prefers their own investing strategy. One of my friends only invests in commercial real estate. Another friend hates real estate because it takes time to look at properties, get funding, and manage the property. He prefers index funds and bonds.

Investing is like philosophy. There are a lot of philosophies and there's no right or wrong way to invest as long as you're achieving results. No matter what you do, make sure you do something that works. Losing money sets you back for years.

Investing is also about expectations. I don't expect to become a full-time investor. I'm a full-time author and entrepreneur. That's my career. I invest some of the money I make in real estate and index funds. That strategy is meant to make me wealthy over the next ten, twenty, thirty years. Not tomorrow. And if you're not ready to invest?

Then don't. Educate yourself, make a living, save your cash, and then act. It's true that starting early is the key to success in investing, but there's also such a thing as starting early and making stupid decisions. By simply avoiding stupid and irresponsible decisions, you will increase your likelihood of becoming wealthy.

"Always plan ahead. It wasn't raining when Noah built the ark."

— *Richard Cushing*

CHAPTER THIRTY-FIVE

EXPLORE WAYS TO GENER-ATE EXTRA INCOME

I never want to rely on one source of income. That's too risky. When you only rely on your salary, you will have no income if you're out of a job. It's the same if you run a business or have a freelancing career. To me, the risk of losing your job or business is not even the worst thing; it's very likely you will find other work so you can pay the bills. **The number one reason I pursue multiple income streams is because it challenges me to become a better person.** You earn money by generating value. And generating value is hard. It took me years to generate real value and make money on my own. For years, I studied, worked for free, and got different jobs. It challenged me to learn more.

I currently keep adding multiple streams of income to build more wealth. I also build multiple income streams to create more variation in my life. The cliché is true, variety makes life a lot more fun. For example, if I don't feel like writing, I can always teach an online course. And if I don't want to do that, I coach entrepreneurs or executives. Or, I can work more at my family business.

Having options makes life fun and free. Remember the "I can always..." technique? If you take that challenge seriously and keep improving the skills you need to do different work, you will always be free to do work you actually enjoy. If you're currently relying on only one income stream, I challenge you to explore all the different ways you can generate extra income. Here are a few ideas:

1. **Start a web-shop**—Sell something you use yourself.

2. **Write and publish a "how-to" book**—Write a book about something you know.

3. **Create a product in 48 hours**—If you want to create a product, give yourself this limitation: What product can I design and get produced within 2 days? You will immediately eliminate 99% of business ideas. Now, only focus on the things you can easily create and sell.

4. **Buy and sell objects you know a lot about**—Buying and selling is the easiest way you can generate cash and help people get what they want. But most people think they can buy and sell anything. I don't believe in that.

5. **Build an app**—If you're a programmer, why not build something yourself?

Try to find ways to generate income without trading your time for money. Becoming an Uber driver or working more hours won't cut it in the long-term. Yes, those things are great to earn more cash so you can start paying off your debt. However, once you're out of debt and doing all right, I challenge you to look beyond trading your time for money. Look for something that's scalable.

Notice that I didn't mention investing on that list? People often say that it takes money to make money. That's true when you have money. But where is that first chunk of money coming from? Exactly, it doesn't appear magically on your bank account. That's what I'm talking about. So before you start thinking about investing your money, find a way to invest your time and skills to *earn* more.

When it comes to generating extra income, focus is the most important thing. You can do thousands of things to make money. But if you chase them all, you will probably not make money with anything. It's tempting to pursue a lot of different things. But to be successful, you want to focus on only a few things. I've often made the mistake of trying different things at the same time. And I always failed. The times I generated the most money and value were the times I was focused on one thing. Know everything about what you do. If you think about it, you can only do that if you focus. It's impossible to know everything about everything. But if you do one thing after the other, anything is possible.

For example, publishing a book can be a good way to earn some extra cash. But writing and publishing a book takes time. During the time you're working on the book, don't chase other opportunities. Finish one project, then, move to the next. That's how I've written six books (counting this one) over the past four years. One after the other. We achieve results sequentially, not simultaneously.

"Someone's sitting in the shade today because someone planted a tree a long time ago."

— Warren Buffet

t

CHAPTER THIRTY-SIX

DECLUTTER YOUR LIFE

My philosophy for material things is this: **The less you own, the better you feel.** I also prefer quality over quantity. I'd rather have one expensive winter coat than two or three cheaper ones. On top of that, I never get attached to objects. Otherwise, you're not truly free. In general, the less you are attached, the freer you are.

Over the years I've become more comfortable with saying goodbye to things: To memories, dreams, goals, people, etc. I think that saying goodbye is a natural part of life. Nothing lasts forever. We all need to get used to it. When my grandmother passed away in 2015, I was surprised by the calm demeanor of my grandfather. I asked him: "Are you not upset?" He said he was sad. But he also told me that as you age, you're forced to say goodbye to people you love.

That's something no one likes. But it's a part of life. And in time, you will get more comfortable with facing reality. However, we don't accept the truth easily. Most of us gradually learn that no matter what happens, you *have* to move on. But you can also train yourself to become better at saying goodbye to things voluntarily. The easiest way to do that is to rid yourself of material possessions. I've found that you can get very attached to stuff that doesn't live. It doesn't matter whether it's a shoe or a person, we can get attached to both.

But in life, we don't have any possessions. Everything is borrowed. That doesn't mean you shouldn't accumulate anything over a lifetime. That's not realistic, and most importantly, it's boring. Who says you *can't* have more than one pair of shoes? Most of us are too busy living life to think about our possessions every single day. I also don't think it's worthwhile to always think about things like:

- "Should I buy this?"
- "Do we need this?"

That requires too much brainpower. Instead, I prefer to do my work, spend time with my friends and family, or go to the gym. I don't want to think about possessions too much. When I see something I truly like, I buy it—since this doesn't happen often, that strategy works well for me. The good thing is that I don't have to overthink things.

it? Go for it. When you keep the things we talked about ... this book in mind (like always seeking the truth, avoiding debt, living below your means), you will be fine. Simply get rid of things when they take up space you need. I regularly donate clothes, shoes, and appliances to charity. And I throw useless things in the trash. I have to tell you, it feels good to live lean. If I don't use something for a few months, it goes out the door. But decluttering your life is more than getting rid of unnecessary stuff. It's about freeing up space in your mind.

Valuable space that you can use for doing useful and meaningful things. Things that you're procrastinating. Decluttering is also an exercise to cope better with loss. Somehow, we have to keep reminding ourselves that everything is borrowed. So, what's catching dust at your home? It's time to roll up your sleeves, grab it by the head, throw it out and say: "Goodbye. I never owned you anyway."

"Nobody really owns anything. We give back our bodies at the end of our lives. We own our thoughts, but everything else is just borrowed. We use it for a while, then pass it on. Everything."

— *Deborah Ellis*

CHAPTER THIRTY-SEVEN

AVOID OVER-PLANNING

Without plans, we will remain trapped by our surroundings. If we don't think about our actions, we will not do the right thing. **But if we plan too much, we might not act.** The purpose of planning is to increase the odds that your actions will be successful. Plans without execution are dreams. When I catch myself planning too much I realize I'm afraid to take action. At some point, you need to settle with your plans; you need to start taking action. And when you start executing your plan, you will find that it has many flaws. Life hardly goes according to plan. There is always something that screws up the best plans. I used to get discouraged by that. "Nothing goes according to plan! Why should I even make plans?" If you have high expectations for your plans and ideas, you will often be disappointed. There's only one solution.

Be prepared for anything, have no expectations, and make the best out of every situation. You simply have to work with the resources you have. A free person has no time to be disappointed. A free person makes a plan and then takes action. And if the plan fails? Draw up another plan. We can't overcomplicate things. There's no time to ask, "What about this? What about that?" Anyone can *make* a plan. Sure, some plans are not thought out well and others are fiercely researched. **But I'd rather execute a good enough plan than never execute the perfect plan.** Because that's what happens to so many of us. You want to be free but you're waiting for the right moment. You need more information. You need to read another book. You need to get another degree. You need more experience. You need more money. You need more moral support.

The truth is that you only need what you *need*. I need nothing. If you adopt that mindset, everything is better than nothing. That doesn't mean you should settle for mediocrity. It simply means you don't need anything. You don't need to wait. Similarly, you don't need to act. If you're content with your life and changed your mindset in a way that you feel free from social restrictions, why would you need more? Just because someone else desires to become financially free, it doesn't mean you need to do the same. Remember, you don't need anything. Sure, you need food and shelter. But that's not what I'm talking about. People who take everything literally are held captive by their negative thoughts. See the bigger picture. If you get your shit together, there's not much you need in life. **Everything is optional.**

Never forget that. I've worked my plans for years. Now, I'm in a place where I have enough money and experience to not worry about food and shelter. Everything I do is optional. I do things because I want to do them. Never make plans or take actions out of fear. That's a recipe for disaster. **Freedom is to do what you want. And if you want something, go and get it.** Your plans will help you to achieve anything that's possible.

Remember to be honest with yourself. If you notice that you're always talking the talk, look inside yourself. Why are you saying something but doing something else? Why are you putting off your dreams? Do you really want it? Or are you trapped in other people's desires? Do you simply want to do something to prove others wrong? Questioning our motives is a part of the planning process. We need to get clear on what we really want. Sometimes we make plans for things we don't even want to do. Why? No one knows. The human mind works in weird ways. Once you've questioned yourself enough and know what you want, take action! That's the only thing that sets you free.

"A good plan today is better than a perfect plan tomorrow."

— *George S. Patton*

CHAPTER THIRTY-EIGHT

FINAL THOUGHTS: THERE'S ALWAYS A WAY OUT

I wrote this book to make you think. I don't want to change the way people think, I want to make them think. *What* you think is up to you. If you think some of my ideas are too die-hard for you, that's fine. My goal is not to convince people that my philosophy for life is the correct one. Life is complex and there's no single best way of living. We all have to create our own strategy for life. One thing we all need to be wary of is self-sabotage. When I talked about the concept of this book with one of my friends, he said:

"But even if I do all the things you do, I'm still not 100% free. I need to pay taxes. I need to get all kinds of permits for everything I want to do. There are so many rules that I can't break. So many responsibilities I can't shake."

I agree, we're never 100% free. And we definitely can't walk away from some responsibilities. For example, as I'm writing this book, my mother has not been well for more than a year. Her health is weak and that is taking a mental toll as well. The way I look at it is that I'm free to support her and stay close to home. I don't look at it as a limitation. Am I free to move to another country? Sure. Do I want that? No, I prefer to support my mother because I want that. It all comes down to the decisions we make.

Understand that some decisions we made in the past will have *permanent* repercussions. If you have a child, it's not noble to detach from your kid. There's also nothing noble about not paying taxes. Screw up once and you'll have to pay the price for a long time—maybe forever. My definition of freedom is a realistic one.

Even if we are obliged to adhere to certain rules, we can still be free to live our life the way we want. As long as we don't break the law, we can do what we want. And if you have a moral code, you will likely never even notice any restrictions. I pay my taxes. If I want to do construction on my house, I will arrange to get a permit. If I made bad decisions in the past, I will face the repercussions from it today. Why? Because I'm free. I'm not tied down by other obligations. On top of that, I *like* to pay taxes. Without rules, our society would not work. The reason we can all live together is because we trust each other. That's how healthy societies function.

I hope you have a good sense of my way of life. I admit it's not perfect. But it works for me. And I hope it will work for you, too. If not, I want to challenge you to keep trying. **No person should ever settle for anything less than freedom. No matter where you are, there is always a way out.** Even if you're restricted in every sense of the word, do not push away your desire to be free. You might be successful for a while. But I firmly believe that no person can remain unfree forever. At some point, our natural desire to be free comes to the surface.

Ultimately, that's the message of this book. **You need to be free to do what you want.** You're privileged to be alive. And no matter what your current circumstance is, you ARE the ruler of your own kingdom. Never accept an unfree life. You can spend your time with the people you love. You can do anything you want. You have power.

But there's a price for all of the above. Are you willing to pay it?

THANK YOU

It means a lot to me that you read this book until the end. I hope you found the ideas useful. If you did, and want to help spreading the word, consider doing one of the following things:

- Talk about freedom with your family, friends, co-workers, or on social media

- Inspire others to be free

- Write a review on Amazon, iBooks, B&N, or your own website

- Buy the paperback for your family, friends, or team

Or anything else you think will help. I'm not asking you to support this book because I'm an independent writer. In fact, I take pride in the fact that the only person I have to answer to is you, my reader.

I don't answer to a publisher, editor or agent. I'm not the type who listens to people who don't have the same intentions as I. I'm here to help others and share the truth. That's why I self-publish my work. I want to be in control. I only listen to my readers. And my readers are the only people who support me.

For that, I say thank you.

If you want to stay in touch or write me an email, sign up to my free newsletter here: http://dariusforoux.com.

-Darius

ACKNOWLEDGEMENTS

I've been thinking about writing this book for two years. But it wasn't until I read *How I Found Freedom In An Unfree World* by Harry Browne, when everything came together. That is such a great book that I recommend everyone to read it. I learned about Harry Browne's book through J.D. Roth's blog GetRichSlowly.org. Thank you for sharing that book, J.D. Without Browne, I probably wouldn't have written the book the way I did.

As I was researching this book, I ran into a website called http://wisdomquotes.com/. Maxime from Montreal, who runs the website, did a great job collecting 400 quotes on freedom. Many of the quotes I shared in this book come from his site. That was very helpful to me.

Finally, I thank my parents for raising me freely. Much of my inspiration comes from the way I was raised. My parents never forced me to do anything. I could always do what I wanted to do. That made me feel responsible. Hence, I always did the right thing. Thank you, Daniel, my brother, for always helping the editing process of all my books and articles until now.

"Liberty is slow fruit. It is never cheap; it is made difficult because freedom is the accomplishment and perfectness of man."

— *Ralph Waldo Emerson*

SPEAKING ENGAGEMENTS

If you are interested in having me speak at your event, company, university, or any other organization, I'm happy to come for free if you buy *What It Takes To Be Free* in bulk.

Books serve as excellent gifts. If you purchase at least 500 copies of my book, I will speak or give a workshop on the topics that I cover for free(read more on dariusforoux.com/speaking). I'd love to discuss ideas in person, in-depth.

Please email me at dariusforoux@gmail.com to tell me about your event/organization and to check my availability.

-Darius

ABOUT THE AUTHOR

Darius Foroux (1987) is the author of 6 books. Since 2015, he's sharing his thoughts about life, business, and productivity on my blog. He also co-founded Vartex, a laundry technology company, while he was finishing my master's degree in Marketing in 2010. For his podcast, The Darius Foroux Show, he's interviewed thought leaders like Ryan Holiday, Cal Newport, Robert Sutton, Jimmy Soni, and more. More books by Darius Foroux:

- Win Your Inner Battles (2016)
- How To Go From Procrastinate Hero to Procrastinate Zero (2016)
- THINK STRAIGHT (2017)
- Do It Today (2018)
- The Road To Better Habits (2019)

Learn more on http://dariusforoux.com/books.

Made in the USA
Coppell, TX
20 October 2022

85014784R00098